The Flower of Chinese Buddhism

Daisaku Ikeda

The Flower of Chinese Buddhism

translated by Burton Watson

New York · WEATHERHILL · *Tokyo*

This book was originally published under the title *Zoku Watakushi no Bukkyokan* (My View of Buddhism, Continued) by Daisan Bummeisha, Tokyo, in 1976.

First edition, 1986
First paperback edition, 1997

Published by Weatherhill, Inc., 568 Broadway, Suite 705, New York, NY 10012. Copyright © 1976, 1986 by Daisaku Ikeda; all rights reserved. Printed in the U.S.A.

Library of Congress Cataloging in Publication Data: Ikeda, Daisaku. / The flower of Chinese Buddhism. / Translation of: . Zoku Watakushi no Bukkyo-kan. / 1. Buddhism–China–History. / I. Title. / BQ 626. I38   1986   294.3'927'0951   86–7826 / ISBN   0–8348–0393–3

Contents

Preface to the English Edition

Ever since I was a child I have felt deeply attracted to China. We Japanese have strong feelings of affinity with China, and I believe this is due not merely to China's geographical proximity, but to the fact that the two nations have been bound by cultural ties over a period of many centuries, and in particular to the fact that Japan received its knowledge of the Buddhist religion primarily from China, a gift for which it owes a debt of gratitude. For the past twenty years or more I have been doing what I could in my small way to bring about the normalization of Sino-Japanese relations and to promote friendship between the peoples of our two countries, and these activities of mine too may in a sense be seen as expressions of the historical ties that link China and Japan.

Speaking from the standpoint of a contemporary Buddhist believer, I have tried in the present work to describe the way in which Buddhism was transmitted from India to China, and how it developed thereafter, outlining the facts and focusing in particular on the personalities involved. I have not attempted to cover the entire history of Chinese Buddhism, however, but have paid special attention to the teachings and translation activities associated with the *Lotus Sutra* because of the connections these have with the Buddhism of Nichiren Daishonin.

In addition to the so-called northern tradition of Buddhism that was transmitted from India to China, and from there to the Korean Peninsula and Japan, there is a second branch of Buddhism, the southern tradition, which spread eastward to Sri Lanka, Burma, and Thailand, and westward toward the Greek and Roman world. But as I observe how the Buddhism of Nichiren Daishonin, which draws upon the northern tradition, is at present transcending boundaries of race and language and spreading throughout the world to become the faith of ever-increasing numbers of people, I cannot help feeling that it is the northern tradition, the history of Chinese Buddhism and its achievements, that will become of real importance from now on.

Dr. Joseph Needham, one of the leading authorities of Western Sinology, states in the preface to his multivolume *Science and Civilisation in China*: "The die is now cast, the world is one. . . . We are living in the dawn of a new universalism, which . . . will unite the working peoples of all races in a community both catholic and cooperative."

This new universalism which Dr. Needham describes must, I feel, be founded upon an outlook that, while fully respecting the individual cultural traditions of the world, thinks ultimately in terms of humankind as a whole. The Chinese tradition often speaks of "studying the old so as to understand the new." In this sense, I believe we have much to learn from the universal spirit displayed in the past by Chinese Buddhism, particularly that which centered about the *Lotus Sutra*, for in this dawn of a new universalism, its accomplishments can undoubtedly contribute to the task of elevating a new sun to the bright zenith of the sky.

I am grateful to Professor Burton Watson, the translator of *The Records of the Historian* and many other works of Chinese literature and history, for undertaking the translation of the present work. I also wish to express my sincere thanks to the members of Weatherhill, Inc., for their efforts in the past and on this occasion in helping to bring my writings before the reading public of the West.

Daisaku Ikeda

Translator's Note

The present volume is a translation of a work in Japanese by Dai-saku Ikeda entitled *Zoku Watakushi no Bukkyokan* ("My View of Buddhism, Continued"; Tokyo: Daisan Bummeisha, 1976). It is designed as a sequel to two earlier works on Buddhism by Mr. Ikeda, translated into English under the titles *The Living Buddha: An Interpretive Biography* (Tokyo: Weatherhill, 1976) and *Buddhism, the First Millennium* (Tokyo: Kodansha International Ltd., 1977). The first is a biography of Shakyamuni Buddha, the founder of the Buddhist religion; the second traces the development of Buddhism in India in the centuries following the death of its founder.

The present volume continues the story of Buddhism's growth and advancement, examining the process by which it was intro-duced to China from the states of India and Central Asia and out-lining its early development on Chinese soil. Mr. Ikeda has not attempted to cover the entire history of Chinese Buddhism down to modern times, nor has he dealt with all the various schools and sects that evolved in China. Instead, after describing the initial stages of Chinese Buddhism, he has chosen to focus his narrative upon those groups that pay special reverence to the *Lotus Sutra,* particularly the T'ien-t'ai Sect, forerunner of the Tendai Sect in Japan, whose complex philosophical doctrines are based upon the teachings of the *Lotus Sutra*. This is the school of Chinese Buddhism that exercised the greatest influence on Nichiren Daishōnin, the

Japanese founder of the sect with which Mr. Ikeda and the other members of the Soka Gakkai are affiliated.

Like Mr. Ikeda's earlier volumes on the history of Buddhism, the original of the present work is in the form of a discussion between Mr. Ikeda and two of his younger associates, but with his permission, I have recast it in straight narrative form for smoother reading. In the chapters dealing with the founders of the T'ien-t'ai Sect, I have supplemented the translation with material drawn from another of Mr. Ikeda's works, *Watakushi no Tendaikan* ("My View of T'ien-t'ai"; Tokyo: Daisan Bummeisha, 1975), and have otherwise made minor changes and adaptations to render the translation more suitable for English readers.

In accordance with earlier practice in the translations in this series, Chinese names and terms are given in the Wade-Giles system of romanization. The more important names, book titles, and terms have been listed in the Appendix, which gives their equivalents in the pinyin system of romanization, their Japanese pronunciation, and other relevant information.

The Flower of Chinese Buddhism

1. From India to China

BUDDHISM AS A WORLD RELIGION

In my earlier volume, *The Living Buddha,* I discussed the life of Shakyamuni, the founder of the Buddhist religion, and in a sequel, *Buddhism, the First Millennium,* I outlined the history of that religion as it developed in India during the first thousand years following Shakyamuni's death. In this, the third volume in the series, I would like to describe the process by which this remarkable religion expanded beyond the borders of India, the country of its birth, spread across Central Asia, and entered China, where it underwent new developments and was eventually transmitted to Korea and Japan.

As I have already pointed out in the preceding volumes, the Buddhism of Shakyamuni was destined not simply to remain a religion of the Indian people alone. Rather, it possessed characteristics of universal appeal that permitted it to transcend national and racial boundaries and present itself as a religion for all humankind. I would like here to focus on the process by which it spread beyond the country of its origin and was received in China, a country with a wholly different cultural background, and see just how that process functioned.

Indian Buddhism falls into two major categories. One is Mahayana Buddhism, sometimes referred to as northern Buddhism because it was the type of Buddhism that in the main spread to the

3

countries to the north and east of India. The other is Theravada or Hinayana Buddhism, sometimes called southern Buddhism, as it was the type that spread to the countries south and east of India such as Sri Lanka, Burma, Thailand, Cambodia, Laos, and Indonesia. Southern Buddhism was also known to some extent in the Greek and Roman worlds to the west of India. Here I propose to concentrate attention on the former, the northern or Mahayana type of Buddhism.

There are several reasons for this decision. First of all, Japan is heir to the Mahayana tradition, and since I am writing from the standpoint of a Japanese Buddhist believer, I would like to throw light on the nature of this Buddhism that has been transmitted to Japan. And in order to understand Mahayana Buddhism, we must observe the manner in which it was transmitted from India to China, and the changes that it underwent in China before being further transmitted to Japan. In addition, I believe that by noting the way in which this religion moved from India, the country of its origin, and spread throughout countries of quite different cultural backgrounds such as China and Japan, we can perceive some of the characteristics that qualify Buddhism as a world religion.

As I have already suggested, the religion of Shakyamuni, when it was transmitted from India to other countries with very different languages and cultures, naturally did not remain unchanged. Though the philosophical core of the religion stayed the same, various adaptations in matters of custom and procedure and various shifts of doctrinal emphasis took place in the new environments into which it was introduced, so that in time China, for example, developed its own distinctive Chinese Buddhism, and the same process was repeated later in Japan.

In this respect, Mahayana Buddhism may be said to differ from the Theravada Buddhism of the southern tradition. Theravada Buddhism as it developed in India and Southeast Asia can be perceived as essentially an extension of the original Buddhism of India. But Mahayana Buddhism, because of the numerous elements introduced into it in the lands to the north and east to which it spread, came to differ so much from Indian Buddhism that it may almost be said to constitute a whole new religion.

My concern here, however, will be not so much with these later elements that were introduced into Mahayana Buddhism as with the fundamental elements that underlie Buddhism of all types, the universals of the religion, as it were. Shortly after Shakyamuni attained enlightenment sitting under the pipal called the Bodhi tree in Buddh Gaya, he determined not to keep his enlightenment to himself but to share it with others. Already, in that moment of decision, Buddhism may be said to have started upon its path of development as a world religion.

In the past, the religion that grew out of Shakyamuni's enlightenment flourished in India and, later, in China and Japan. But because this religion addressed itself to the problems of birth, old age, sickness, and death, problems that face every living person, it is in my opinion by no means destined to remain a religion of the East Asian and Southeast Asian peoples alone. Today we see Buddhism spreading to the continents of Australia, Africa, Europe, North America, and South America, and I am confident that this process will continue in the future. What we want to try to clarify here, therefore, is the way in which Buddhism in the past has spread from country to country and how it has come to attain its status as a world religion.

In examining the history of this process of diffusion, I will be writing from the standpoint of a Buddhist believer of the present age, as I have done in the previous volumes in this series. My aim, therefore, is not to delve into all the various aspects of the development of Buddhism in India and the lands to which it was transmitted or to try to describe in detail the countless scholarly studies that have been carried out on the subject. Rather, as I survey the history of Buddhism in India, China, and Japan, I will be seeking always to discover what is the real essence of the Buddhist religion, what is the spirit, the vital spark in it that enables it to go on living and growing today.

THE INTRODUCTION OF BUDDHISM TO CHINA

In the past, the commonly accepted account of the introduction of Buddhism to China placed that event in the tenth year of the Yung-p'ing era of the reign of Emperor Ming of the Later Han dynasty (A.D. 25–220), a date that corresponds to A.D. 67 by the Western calendar. Though there are different theories concerning the dates of Shakyamuni's birth and death, if we assume that he died around 486 B.C., the religion he founded was introduced to China about five hundred years after his passing.

According to these accounts, Emperor Ming dreamed of a golden man of unusual height flying in the air in front of his palace. Questioning his ministers as to the meaning of the dream, he was told that the golden man was the Buddha. He thereupon dispatched envoys to the regions west of China to seek knowledge of the Buddhist religion. The account goes on to state that the envoys dispatched by Emperor Ming eventually reached the land of the Yüeh-chih people in northern India, where they encountered two Buddhist monks named Chia-she Mo-t'eng and Chu Fa-lan. From them they obtained Buddhist images and sutras running to six hundred thousand words, which they loaded on a white horse. Then, with the Buddhist monks accompanying them, they returned to the Han capital at Lo-yang and settled down in a government office outside the western gate of the capital, in buildings that in time came to be known as the White Horse Temple. The Buddhist images are symbolic of the Buddha, the sutras of the Law or Dharma, and the two monks of the Order, and thus, according to this account, the so-called Three Treasures of Buddhism, the Buddha, the Law, and the Order, were officially introduced to China for the first time.

This famous account, which appears in slightly different form in a number of early Chinese works, has in recent years been subjected to vigorous attack. Scholars have pointed out numerous anachronisms and inconsistencies in it and have concluded that it is purely legendary in nature and cannot be accepted as historical fact. We are not so much interested, however, in discovering just when the Buddhist religion was formally introduced to the Chinese ruler and his court—be it Emperor Ming or some other sovereign— than in learning when its teachings first reached the nameless masses of people in China and brought to them a message of salvation from the pains of life and of sickness, old age, and death. But because of the enormous prestige of the imperial institution in China and the role played by the government in fostering the writing of history and the keeping of official records, the written accounts preserved from early China tend to focus principally upon the lives and actions of the emperor and the ruling class and to take little notice of the lot of the common people. Therefore we must be content with what information can be gleaned from such records, while surmising what we can about the manner in which the teachings of Buddhism spread among the Chinese populace as a whole.

In this connection, there is evidence to indicate that Prince Ying of Ch'u, a younger half-brother of Emperor Ming of the Han dynasty, paid honor to the Buddhist religion. According to his biography in *The History of the Later Han,* in his youth he was fond of wandering knights and adventurers and entertained a number of guests and visitors at his residence. It is probable that among the latter were monks or merchants from foreign countries who brought him news of the Buddhist religion. In his later years he displayed a great fondness for the study of the Taoist doctrines of the Yellow Emperor and Lao Tzu and "made offerings and paid honor to *fou-t'u.*" The term *fou-t'u* has been identified by scholars as a Chinese phonetic transcription of the word Buddha.

In the eighth year of the Yung-p'ing era (A.D. 65), Emperor Ming issued an edict permitting persons who had been accused of crimes calling for the death penalty to ransom themselves by payment of a certain number of rolls of silk to the government. Prince Ying of Ch'u, apparently suffering from an uneasy conscience because of something he had done, submitted thirty roles of silk to the throne, claiming that he had committed numerous faults and evil deeds in the past. The emperor, however, issued a statement saying that there was no need for such a payment and praising

his younger brother for, among other things, "honoring the benevolent altars of the Buddha and fasting and purifying himself
for a period of three months." He accordingly returned the ransom,
instructing that it be used to prepare sumptuous feasts for the
upasakas (Buddhist laymen) and *shramanas* (monks) in the region.

This brief episode, recorded in the prince's biography in the
official history of the dynasty, *The History of the Later Han,* not only
tells us that a younger brother of the emperor paid homage to Buddhist images, but that there were Buddhist monks and lay believers
residing in his territory, all of this previous to the year A.D. 67, when
the legend of Emperor Ming and the golden man says that Buddhism was first introduced to China.

The region of Ch'u, the fief assigned to Prince Ying, was situated
southeast of Lo-yang, with its capital at P'eng-ch'eng. Prince Ying
was enfeoffed as nominal ruler of the region in A.D. 52, having
previously lived in the capital, Lo-yang. It is quite possible that he
had already learned about Buddhism while he was in Lo-yang and
had begun his worship of Buddhist images at that time. If not, then
we must suppose that Buddhism, after entering China from the
west, had already spread as far as the region of Ch'u, where the
prince became acquainted with it after going there in A.D. 52.

Another important point to note in this account of Prince Ying
is the fact that the emperor, in his proclamation concerning the
matter, expresses open approval of the worshipping of Buddhist
images and the giving of alms and support to followers of the Buddhist religion. If the document is to be believed, then already in
the time of Emperor Ming the ruling house of China was prepared
to accord open sanction to the practices of Buddhism.

Chapter 108 of *The History of the Later Han,* "The Account of the
Western Regions," in the section on India relates the story of
Emperor Ming's dream of the golden man and says, "The emperor
thereupon dispatched envoys to India to inquire about the Way
of the Buddha, and in time [Buddhist] images were painted in
China. Prince Ying of Ch'u was the first to place his belief in its
teachings, and thereafter in China there were many persons who
honored its doctrines." This passage too would seem to confirm

the assumption that the Buddhist faith first took root in China in the time of Emperor Ming.

The History of the Later Han was written by Fan Yeh (398–445), who lived some three or four hundred years after the events that he describes. It is therefore not surprising that the few brief accounts that he gives concerning the introduction of Buddhism to China should show the influence of popular legends such as that describing Emperor Ming's dream of the golden man. However, his remarks, though perhaps not entirely reliable as history, would seem to indicate that Emperor Ming showed a considerable appreciation of the teachings of Buddhism, and it is probably no accident that the introduction of Buddhism has traditionally come to be associated with the name of that ruler.

Moreover, if, as the biography of Prince Ying indicates, there was already in the first century A.D. a member of the imperial family who placed faith in the Buddhist teachings, then it is only natural to suppose that the new religion had by this time won a certain number of converts among the populace as a whole. A knowledge of Buddhism was probably brought to China by merchants and travelers from other lands who journeyed to China over the Silk Road, the trade route linking China with Central Asia and the countries to the west. If this supposition is correct, then a knowledge of Buddhism must have reached the western portions of China first and from there spread to Lo-yang and the regions such as Ch'u to the east.

Possible Earlier Contacts with Buddhism

In addition to the accounts described above, there have been various legends or speculations that would push the date for the introduction of Buddhism to China back to an earlier period. India in the third century B.C. was headed by the powerful monarch King Ashoka, the third ruler of the Maurya dynasty, who was an enthusiastic supporter of Buddhism and who sent missionaries to the surrounding countries to spread its teachings. His reign corresponds roughly to that of Ch'in Shih Huang-ti, the head of a feudal state who succeeded in uniting all of China under his rule and in 221 B.C. declared himself First Emperor of the Ch'in dynasty, which lasted from 255 to 206 B.C. Under these powerful and dynamic monarchs, both India and China were expanding their borders and reaching out toward each other. It is not surprising, therefore, that Chinese Buddhists in later ages should have speculated that missionaries from King Ashoka's court reached China and introduced the Buddha's teachings. Traditional accounts of King Ashoka assert that he erected eighty-four thousand stupas to enshrine the relics of the Buddha. The *Ming Fo Lun,* a work by the Chinese scholar and painter Tsung Ping (375–443), states that some of these stupas were discovered in the Shantung and Shansi regions of China and, when opened, were found to contain Buddhist relics.

According to another Chinese work, the *Li-tai San-pao Chi* by Fei Ch'ang-fang, completed in 597, a party of foreign Buddhist monks reached China in the time of the First Emperor of the Ch'in, but the emperor had them thrown into prison. It also asserts that a monk named Shih Li-fang and a number of other worthy persons brought Buddhist sutras to China in the time of the First Emperor. The emperor refused to listen to their teachings and eventually placed them in confinement, but they were freed by a miraculous being who appeared at night and broke open the prison walls. Because of the late date of the works in which these assertions appear and the supernatural elements mingled in them it is difficult, however, to regard them as anything more than pious legends.

Other sources would date the introduction of Buddhism to China to the time of another powerful Chinese ruler, Emperor Wu of the Former Han dynasty (206 B.C.–A.D. 25), who reigned from 140 to 87 B.C. Emperor Wu dispatched an envoy named Chang Ch'ien to travel to the regions west of China and learn what he could about the peoples living there. Chang Ch'ien returned to China in 126 B.C. with eyewitness accounts of a number of states in Central Asia and reports of lands farther afield such as India, Parthia, and the Roman Empire. The "Treatise on Buddhism and Taoism" in *The History of the Wei,* by Wei Shou, compiled shortly after A.D.

520, goes so far as to state that, as a result of Chang Ch'ien's mission, "the teachings of the Buddha were for the first time heard of." We may note, however, that the earlier accounts of Chang Ch'ien's mission in *The Records of the Historian* by Ssu-ma Ch'ien (145?–90? B.C.) or *The History of the Former Han* by Pan Ku (A.D. 32–92) make no mention of Buddhist teachings.

Shortly after the time of Chang Ch'ien's mission, in 121 B.C., Emperor Wu sent one of his most trusted generals, Ho Ch'ü-ping, on an expedition against the Hsiung-nu, a nomadic people who lived in the desert regions north of China and from time to time plundered the Chinese border area. In the course of capturing or killing various Hsiung-nu leaders, Ho Ch'ü-ping came into possession of a "golden man" that one of the Hsiung-nu leaders was said to have used in worshipping Heaven. This much of the story is recorded in the earlier and more reliable histories such as those mentioned above. The "Treatise on Buddhism and Taoism," however, goes on to state that Emperor Wu, regarding the image as that of a great deity, installed it in the Palace of Sweet Springs, where he burned incense before it and worshipped it. "This, then," says the "Treatise on Buddhism and Taoism," "was the modest beginning of the influx of the Way of the Buddha."[1]

In view of the fact that a "golden man" figures in the famous legend of Emperor Ming's dream, it is understandable that Chinese Buddhists should have supposed that this earlier golden man of the Hsiung-nu leader likewise had some connection with Buddhism. Modern scholars, however, after examining the evidence, have concluded that the image captured from the Hsiung-nu could not have been Buddhist in nature.

All of this, of course, does not prove that a knowledge of Buddhism had not in fact reached China in the time of the First Emperor of the Ch'in or of Emperor Wu of the Han—merely that no reliable notice of that fact is to be found in the Chinese written re-

---

1. *Wei Shou, Treatise on Buddhism and Taoism,* Leon Hurvitz tr., in *Yün-kang, the Buddhist Cave-Temples of the Fifth century A.D. in North China,* vol. 16, Kyoto University, 1956.

cords of the period. But there are several reasons why I believe that, even if Buddhist monks had actually reached China before the first century A.D. or reports of the Buddhist religion had been transmitted to the Chinese, it is unlikely that Buddhism could have attracted much attention or spread very widely in China at that time.

The First Emperor of the Ch'in is well known as an enthusiastic supporter of the school of philosophy known as Legalism, which urged the creation of a strong bureaucratic state and the governing of the people through a detailed and stringent system of laws and penalties. In an attempt to enforce allegiance to Legalist doctrines, the First Emperor in 213 B.C. carried out his infamous "Burning of the Books," ordering the suppression of other systems of thought such as Confucianism and the destruction of their writings. In such a totalitarian atmosphere, it is unlikely that a foreign religion such as Buddhism, had it been introduced to China, would have been given a fair or sympathetic reception. It is interesting to note that, even in the Buddhist anecdotes concerning the First Emperor of the Ch'in that have been mentioned above, the emperor figures as a persecutor of the newly introduced religion rather than a supporter of it.

Though there was somewhat greater freedom of thought during the Han dynasty, we should note that Emperor Wu took steps to make Confucianism the official creed of the state and to encourage the study and practice of its doctrines. In later centuries, Confucianism was to prove one of the most powerful and persistent opponents of the Buddhist religion in China, and therefore we cannot help but surmise that a period of strong Confucian influence such as that of Emperor Wu would hardly have been a propitious time for the introduction and promulgation of Buddhist teachings.

Moreover, the period represented by the reigns of the First Emperor of the Ch'in and the early Han rulers such as Emperor Wu was one of territorial expansion and great cultural pride and self-confidence. At such a time, the characteristic Chinese tendency to view native ideas and institutions as superior and to look down on those of other countries would naturally have been at its strongest. This is another reason why it seems unlikely that Buddhism could have made much progress in China at this time even if it had been introduced.

A highly complex and philosophical religion such as Buddhism requires a considerable period of sympathetic trial and study before it can be fully understood by the people of any new country to which it is introduced. In this respect, it differs from those less highly developed religions which, arising on the popular level, enjoy a certain period of frenzied vogue but quickly die out. Regardless of what knowledge the Chinese may have had of the Indian religion in the centuries before the official notices of its introduction, we may say with certainty that the first real period of Buddhist study and propagation in China did not begin until the first and second centuries A.D.

The Situation in Central Asia

We do not know for certain just when or how Buddhism entered China. It is possible that it was transmitted directly from India by persons journeying to China by sea. But it appears much more likely that, as the legend of Emperor Ming's dream suggests, it was introduced from the countries of Central Asia by Chinese envoys or foreign missionaries traveling over the so-called Silk Road that linked China with the West. Let us therefore see what the situation was in these Central Asian states around the time when Buddhism was believed to have first entered China.

By the time in question, the Buddhist religion had already spread from India to the states of Central Asia, perhaps, as the accounts suggest, through the efforts of missionaries sent out by King Ashoka. There the Indian religion underwent certain changes before being passed on to China. These states hence played the role of intermediaries in transmitting the religion from its country of origin to China and the other lands of East Asia. We see evidence of that role in the fact that a number of important Buddhist terms such as *sha-men* (*shramana* or recluse) and *ch'u-chia* (monk) seem to have derived not directly from Sanskrit words but from terms used in the languages of the Central Asian states. In addition, the Chinese terms for the links in the so-called twelvefold chain of causation, which constitutes one of the basic philosophical principles of Buddhism, appear to have been translated from some Tocharian language of Central Asia.

We know that as a result of cultural contacts between China and Central Asia brought about by the opening of the Silk Road a number of new plants and foods were introduced to China. The Chinese indicated the foreign origin of such imports by attaching the term *hu* or "barbarian," to the name, as in *hu-ma,* "barbarian hemp," the Chinese term for sesame; *hu-kua,* "barbarian melon," or cucumber; and *hu-t'ao,* "barbarian peach," or walnut. If new foods of this type were being disseminated by merchants and travelers passing over the Silk Road, it is easy to imagine that items of nonmaterial culture as well, such as the Buddhist religion, were also finding their way into China by the same route.

The historian Ssu-ma Ch'ien, in his "Account of Ta-yüan" (*Records of the Historian* 123), had described the visits of Chang Ch'ien and others to such Central Asian states as Ferghana, Bactria, and the region of the Great Yüeh-chih people. Pan Ku, in his "Account of the Western Regions" (*Former Han* 96), which deals with the same area, describes not only the Silk Road leading west to the land of the Great Yüeh-chih and Parthia, but a second road that branched off and led to the regions of Chi-pin (Kashmir) and Wu-i-shan-li (Arachosia). Kashmir and Arachosia were areas of northeastern India in which Buddhism was at this time well established and flourishing. If a road connected these regions with China, it is not difficult to imagine that merchants or Buddhist believers traveling over that road could have brought word of Buddhism to the people of China.

We have already made several references to the Great Yüeh-chih people of Central Asia. In this connection, one more important notice concerning Buddhism to be found in early Chinese sources remains to be mentioned, that in the work known as *A Brief Account of the Wei,* which was compiled by Yü Huan during the period from 239 to 265. The *Brief Account of the Wei* is no longer extant as a separate work, but fortunately it is quoted extensively in the commentary that P'ei Sung-chih wrote to *The Record of the Three Kingdoms*. At the end of chapter 30 of the "Wei Annals" section of *The Three Kingdoms*, there is an extended quotation from the "Account of the Western Barbarians" of the *Brief Account of the Wei* which, in a passage on the state of Lin-erh, or Lumbini, in Nepal, describes the birth of the Buddha and gives the names of his father and mother. It then goes on to state: "In the past, in the reign of Emperor Ai of the Han, the first year of the Yüan-shou era (2 B.C.), the Erudite Disciple Ching-lu received the oral transmission of the Buddhist scriptures from I-ts'un, an envoy of the king of the Great Yüeh-chih."

Because of the accurate and fairly detailed knowledge of Buddhism which Yü Huan displays in this passage, the account has been highly regarded by scholars and constitutes one of our most valuable early pieces of information on the introduction of Buddhism to China. True, it does not tell us where the act of oral transmission, the usual way of spreading the teachings at this time, took place, or what consequences came of it, but it does give us a definite date for the transaction.

The Yüeh-chih were a nomadic people who, when first heard of, lived in the region just west of China. Later they were defeated by the Hsiung-nu, another nomadic people, and driven much farther to the west. There they conquered the region of Bactria and set up their own kingdom. Around the beginning of the first century A.D., they greatly expanded the territory under their control, moving into the area of present-day Afghanistan and Pakistan and establishing a dynasty known as the Kushana dynasty. They also brought under their control the area of Gandhara, which had previously been ruled by Greek kings, and established their capital there at a site corresponding to the present-day Peshawar.

The Yüeh-chih people, or Kushanas, as they are known in Indian history, had by this time become followers of Buddhism and, as we have seen above, played a role in transmitting a knowledge of the religion to China. The most famous of the Kushana rulers was the third king, Kanishka, who probably lived during the first half of the second century. A fervent patron of Buddhism, he called together the Fourth Buddhist Council to put the sacred texts in order and carried out other steps to encourage the spread of the religion. It was at this time that Greek artistic influences from the preceding period combined with themes of the Buddhist religion to produce the realistic depictions of the Buddha and his followers that are characteristic of Gandharan art. It may also be noted that the coins of the Kushana dynasty frequently bore images of the Buddha.

Bactria, the region where the Yüeh-chih people had resided formerly, was believed to have been dominated by the Zoroastrian religion. But excavations carried out there around 1960 have unearthed a number of inscriptions dealing with King Ashoka and have made clear that as early as the third century B.C. it was a part of the Buddhist world. It is likely, therefore, that the Yüeh-chih people became converts to Buddhism during their stay in that area, and this conversion laid the foundation for the flourishing Buddhism of the Kushana dynasty. Along with the reign of King Ashoka, the Kushana dynasty represents one of the peaks of Buddhist influence and cultural activity in Indian history. And, as we shall see in the next chapter, monk-translators from the region of the Great Yüeh-chih, as the Chinese termed it, played a key role in transmitting a knowledge of the Buddhist scriptures to China.

2. Early Chinese Translations
of Buddhist Scriptures

Seeking Knowledge of Buddhism

In the preceding chapter I have discussed the way in which, so far as can be surmised from the evidence, Buddhism spread from India, passed along the Silk Road running through Central Asia, and was introduced to China. In terms of the Western calendar, these events probably took place around the first century B.C. and the first century A.D. I would like next to focus attention on the activities of the Buddhist monks and believers who came to China from the region of Central Asia in the period from the first to the fourth centuries A.D. and were active in the task of making Chinese translations of Buddhist scriptures and commentaries.

Perhaps the most famous translators of Buddhist scriptures into Chinese were Kumarajiva, Paramartha, Hsüan-tsang and Pu-k'ung, who have come to be known as the Four Great Monk-Translators of Scripture. But these figures all lived in the period from the fifth to the eighth century, and for that reason, and because their importance demands rather detailed discussion, I will treat them in later chapters. Here let us consider for a moment the men who preceded them and who first took up the difficult task of putting the more important Buddhist texts into Chinese.

The first problem that faced these men from Central Asia who were attempting to convey a knowledge of Buddhism to the Chinese was that there were no schools for language training such as we have today and scarcely any dictionaries that could aid them in their work. At first they probably had to speak in very broken language and use gestures to eke out the meaning, striving in whatever way they could to make clear to the Chinese the content of the Buddhist teachings. We must keep in mind that although China had been in contact with the countries of Central Asia since the second century B.C., the cultural exchanges that had taken place consisted mainly of diplomatic missions exchanged between China and the Central Asian countries or of merchant groups traveling back and forth. It must have required a considerable period of time before anything so complex and profound as the Buddhist writings and the uniquely Indian concepts and modes of thought underlying them could be adequately introduced and explained to the Chinese.

We have noted in the preceding chapter the account of how the Chinese court scholar Ching-lu received oral instruction in the Buddhist scriptures from I-ts'un, an envoy of the king of the Great Yüeh-chih people. But it seems unlikely that a Chinese scholar trained in Confucian doctrine, without any previous background or experience in Buddhism or Indian thought, could have gained a very profound understanding of Buddhist doctrine in that manner. Moreover, though Prince Ying of the state of Ch'u was said to have worshipped the Buddha as early as A.D. 65, he seems to have revered the Buddha in the same way he did the Yellow Emperor and Lao Tzu, traditional figures of the native Taoist tradition. He and others like him at the time who had some knowledge of Buddhism probably prayed to the Buddha as they prayed to the deities of the Taoist pantheon, in hopes of acquiring supernatural powers or attaining the status of an immortal spirit.

The Buddhist images imported from Central Asia at first were probably prized mainly as rare and unusual works of art and treated with reverence for that reason. Though this is no more than conjecture, we may surmise that it was only later that the possessors of such images began to realize the depth and complexity of the symbolism underlying the images and to take an interest in the teachings of Buddhism.

The Chinese who felt moved to learn more about Buddhism naturally turned for instruction to the monks from Central Asia who had made their way to China and taken up residence there. Such monks were referred to by the Chinese as *hu-seng*, "barbarian monks," or *sang-men*, the latter term a transcription of the Sanskrit word *shramana*, meaning a recluse or religious practitioner. These immigrant monks from Central Asia no doubt acquired some degree of fluency in the Chinese language in the course of their years in China. And, out of their desire to propagate the teachings of their religion, they would naturally respond with fervor to the Chinese who came to them seeking a deeper understanding of Buddhism.

To be sure, there were a certain number of Chinese officials attached to the government who were proficient in the languages of Central Asia and might have been of assistance in furthering Chinese knowledge of Buddhism. But their duty was to act as interpreters when diplomatic exchanges took place between China and the states of Central Asia and to prepare official records of such exchanges. They would hardly have had the time or inclination to engage in an undertaking such as the translation of the Buddhist sacred texts into Chinese. That was not an officially sponsored enterprise, but one undertaken by the monks from Central Asia in response to the sincere desire of the Chinese to learn more about this remarkable religion that had been introduced to their country.

In the preceding chapter we have noted the various accounts concerning the initial introduction of Buddhism to China. But it was a century or a century and a half before the task of translating the scriptures into Chinese began in earnest. In the reign of Emperor Huan of the Later Han, which lasted from 146 to 167, the task was initiated by An Shih-kao, a Parthian monk who arrived in Lo-yang in 148, and carried on by later arrivals such as the Yüeh-chih monk Chih Lou-chia-ch'an, or Lokaraksha.

According to the official history of the period, Emperor Huan performed sacrifices in the palace to the Taoist deities Lao Tzu and the Yellow Emperor and to the Buddha and was probably a man of deep religious faith. He took measures to assist the monk-translators from Central Asia and carried out various other religious activities. We may surmise that it was around this time that Buddhism began to exercise a concrete influence on Chinese society.

Before a religion imported from abroad can take root in a society and begin to gain general acceptance, a considerable period of trial and tentative acceptance is required. This is particularly true in the case of a conservative society such as ancient China, which took great pride in its past and tended to look down on the culture and civilization of other countries.

There appears to be a gap of a hundred years or more between the time when Buddhism was said to have been introduced to China and the period when serious translation of the sacred texts began. But we may be certain that during that period many foreign monks and their Chinese converts, whose names have now been lost to us, were working diligently to spread word of the Buddhist teachings among the population. They undoubtedly faced great obstacles in their work, hampered by language barriers and the lack of adequate translations of the Buddhist scriptures. Moreover, though Confucianism was in a period of decline at the time, it was still the officially sanctioned philosophy of the state, and its supporters no doubt looked down upon Buddhism as a religion of foreign barbarians and took what steps they could to hinder the endeavors of its propagators and converts. Thus much time and labor was required to reach the point where Buddhism gained open acceptance and enjoyed the patronage of rulers such as Emperor Huan.

Though history provides no details of the men and women who worked to propagate Buddhism in China in this initial period or just how the religion spread and grew, we may be certain that if there had not been much hard and persistent labor on the lower levels, if there had not been powerful underground streams flowing among the populace, Buddhism could not have risen so rapidly to a place of great importance in Chinese society, could not have become the surging river of faith that it did become when the activities of the Buddhist monks and propagators make their appearance in the historical records during the reign of Emperor Huan. In this sense, this initial period, though we have pitifully little information about it, was one of major importance in the history of Chinese Buddhism as a whole.

MONK-TRANSLATORS FROM CENTRAL ASIA

Standing in the way of Chinese translation of the Buddhist scriptures were the formidable barriers of language that separated the Indian and Chinese civilizations. But we must keep in mind that there were also geographical barriers separating the two countries. As mentioned earlier, the fervent believers of the countries of Central Asia worked to overcome these physical barriers and transmit the teachings of Buddhism to China. If it had not been for their mediating role, Buddhism might never have reached China and the other lands to the east of it, and the place of Central Asian Buddhists in the history of East Asian Buddhism is thus a major one.

China and India, in company with ancient Egypt and Mesopotamia farther to the west, rank as the four great cradles of human civilization. But though China and India are both part of the same general sphere of Asian culture, they are separated by the Himalayas, ranges of mountains so lofty and rugged that they have been labeled the roof of the world. Since these mountains virtually block off all contact between the two countries, if Buddhism was to be transmitted from India to China, it had to be carried either on a roundabout route north to the region of Central Asia and then east to China, or over the southern sea route from India to the China coast. Either route was fraught with peril, and anyone embarking upon such a journey must have known that he was taking his life in his hands.

In Han times, when Buddhism was first introduced to China, little or no mention is made of the sea route, and we can only speculate what attempts may have been made to travel it. With regard to the overland route, however, we know that from the time of Emperor Wu (the latter part of the second century B.C.) the Chinese rulers in reign after reign worked to open up communications with the countries to the west, and the histories of the period preserve accounts of the roads to the region of Central Asia and the travelers who journeyed over them.

This overland route, though it avoided the perils of a sea voyage, was beset with great difficulties of its own. Anyone traveling east on it from India to China had first to cross the Pamir Mountains. At Kashgar at the eastern foot of the Pamirs, the route split into two roads, one passing east along the northern edge of the Taklamakan Desert, the other passing along the southern edge. To the north of the desert were the peaks of the Tien Shan Mountains, while to the south ran the Kunlun range. Moving from one sparse oasis to another, travelers were barely able to make their way across the desert wastes.

The Chinese monk Fa-hsien, who traveled west across the desert in A.D. 399, wrote that "the sands are full of evil spirits and burning winds, and anyone who encounters them dies; no one is left unharmed. No birds fly overhead, no animals run across the ground. Squint one's eyes, gaze as one may in the four directions, he can find no place to turn to, nothing to guide him; only the dried bones of the dead serve as markers of the trail."

The first persons to venture into this barren and forbidding region were probably the military men and explorers sent out by Emperor Wu of the Han. In his efforts to strengthen China and check the power of the nomadic Hsiung-nu tribes to the north, the emperor sought to establish an alliance with the Yüeh-chih. In addition, he was eager to obtain horses from the Central Asian state of Ta-yüan, or Ferghana, which was famous for its so-called blood-sweating horses. To accomplish these aims, he repeatedly dispatched armies and envoys to Central Asia. States that attempted to resist the advance of the imperial armies, such as the little kingdom of Lou-lan, were attacked and overthrown, and large numbers of fighting men on both sides left their bones to bleach in the shifting sands. The Japanese novelist Yasushi Inoue has written of the events of the period in his story entitled *Lou-lan*.

This route through the region of Central Asia, as we have seen, came in time to be referred to as the Silk Road, and the second group of persons to pass over it were merchants in the silk trade. They knew that Chinese silk goods could be sold for a very high price in Persia and the Roman Empire, and they set off with their caravans to cross the desert in search of profit. Needless to say, they also brought back to China various rarities from the western regions such as precious stones and the famous jade produced by the Central Asian state of Khotan. Spurred on by the prospect of the huge monetary gains to be gotten from the East-West trade, they set off over the snowy mountains and the swift flowing streams and, like so many travelers on the route, often perished along the way.

The third group to pass over the road were the Buddhist missionaries. But unlike the groups that preceded them, they were not urged by dreams of political conquest or material gain. They had already abandoned all thought of worldly fame or profit, and burned only with religious ardor, determined to carry the teachings of their faith to the peoples of other lands. Thus they were prepared to face any dangers and hardships in the pursuit of their goal. Some of them doubtless perished on the road, their strength exhausted in the forbidding desert wastes while China was still far beyond the eastern horizon. But others surmounted the difficulties and were able to reach their destination. Having resolved from the beginning that they would never see their native lands again, they settled down there, adopted Chinese ways, and devoted the remainder of their lives to the propagation of the faith. Unlike the earlier soldiers and merchants, they passed over the Silk Road only once and thereafter gave themselves up wholly to religious concerns. Difficult as the journey to China must have been, the task that confronted the missionaries there in some ways posed an even greater problem, that of how to transmit the Buddhist doctrine to people of a totally different race, language, and culture. As a step in the direction of solving this problem, they undertook the important job of translating various of the Buddhist scriptures into Chinese.

The first Buddhist missionaries to journey over the Silk Road to China were nearly all from the states of Central Asia rather than from India itself. It was not until some time later that missionaries from India traveled in any significant numbers to China. In this early period, it was customary to prefix a word indicating what country the missionary came from to his Chinese name. Earlier we have mentioned An Shih-kao, the Parthian monk who arrived in China in A.D. 147. The element *an* in his name is an abbreviation for An-hsi, the Chinese name for the state of Parthia, which was founded around 250 B.C. in the region of present-day Iran. An Shih-kao was a prince of the royal family of Parthia. On the death of his father, the king of Parthia, he relinquished his right to the throne to his younger brother and gave himself up to the study of Buddhism. After traveling to various Central Asian states, he journeyed to China in 147, and there spent more than twenty years translating Buddhist texts into Chinese and propagating their doctrines. The element *chih* in the names of Chih Lou-chia-ch'an and Chih Yüeh (who, like An Shih-kao, arrived in China in the latter part of the Later Han dynasty), Chih Ch'ien (who arrived in the succeeding Three Kingdoms period, 221–65) or Chih Shih-lun (who arrived in the time of the Eastern Chin dynasty, 317–420) indicates that they were natives of the state of Kushana (Yüeh-chih) or that their forebears were natives of that state.

Chu Fa-hu, a monk who in 286 completed a translation of the *Lotus Sutra* entitled *Cheng Fa-hua Ching,* was of Yüeh-chih descent. Born in Tun-huang in far western China, he is sometimes referred to as the Tun-huang Bodhisattva or as Chih Fa-hu, the Yüeh-chih Bodhisattva, because of his descent. His teacher, however, was an Indian monk named Chu Kao-tso, the *chu* element standing for T'ien-chu, one of the Chinese names for India. Fa-hu, though he himself was not Indian, simply adopted the *chu* element from his teacher's name and prefixed it to his own name as though it were a surname.

Similarly, the element *k'ang* prefixed to the names of K'ang Meng-hsiang and K'ang Seng-k'ai indicates that these monks were natives of or descendants of natives of K'ang-chü, or Sogdiana, a state in the area of present-day Samarkand that was an important center of Buddhist activity.

Although these various states of Central Asia were alike in paying allegiance to the Buddhist faith, they differed in the particular type of Buddhism that they embraced. Some seem to have studied both southern or Hinayana Buddhism and northern or Mahayana Buddhism. But the general tendency was to embrace one or the other and adhere to that exclusively. An Shih-kao, the monk from Parthia, for example, translated only Hinayana texts such as the *Sutra of the Four Noble Truths,* the *Sutra of the Eightfold Path,* and the *Sutra of the Turning of the Wheel of the Law.* By contrast, Lokaraksha, who came from Kushana, gave his attention mainly to Mahayana texts such as the *Prajnaparamita Sutra in Eight Thousand Lines,* the *Pan-chou San-mei Ching,* and the *Shuramgama Sutra.* This would seem to indicate that the Kushana kingdom paid honor to the Mahayana teachings.

In any event, there is no doubt that Buddhism flourished greatly in these states of Central Asia from around the first century B.C. and A.D. until the time of Islamic expansion in the area in the seventh century. The Chinese monks Fa-hsien in his *Record of Buddhist Countries* and Hsüan-tsang in his *Record of the Western Region in the Time of the Great T'ang* have left us firsthand accounts of the thriving condition of Buddhism based on their observations when they passed through the area on their way to India. In Han times it had been customary to speak of the thirty-six states of the Hsi-yü, or Western Region, as the Chinese termed the area of Central Asia, but by the period of Fa-hsien and Hsüan-tsang the number of states had swelled to over fifty.

According to scholars in the field, the leaders of these Central Asian states were an Aryan people of Iranian stock. All of them spoke some language belonging to the Indo-European family of languages and it is therefore likely that they could read the Buddhist scriptures in the original Sanskrit or Pali. But translations of

Buddhist works into Khotanese, the language of the Central Asian oasis state of Khotan, have been found, so we know that some translation activity took place. Still, the languages of India and Central Asia were close enough so that translation from Sanskrit or Pali into one of the Central Asian languages did not present any great problems.

Such, however, was not the case when Buddhism was transmitted to China and the scriptures had to be translated into a language belonging to a wholly different language family, the Sino-Tibetan family. Chinese is totally different in structure from Sanskrit and Pali, the languages of the Buddhist scriptures. Moreover, while the Indian languages use a phonetic system of writing, Chinese employs a system that is mainly ideographic. Hence it was unrealistic to expect ordinary Chinese to learn to read the Buddhist scriptures in Sanskrit or Pali, and it became absolutely necessary to translate them into Chinese if the religion was to have any chance of widespread acceptance. The monks of Central Asia served as mediators between the Chinese and Indian language spheres, using their knowledge of the languages of both areas to overcome the barriers that stood in the way of the propagation of the faith.

A PRICELESS CULTURAL LEGACY

The labor of translating the Buddhist sutras and other writings into Chinese, which began in the time of Emperor Huan of the Later Han, continued until the time of the Northern Sung dynasty (960–1125), covering a period of almost a thousand years. Japan since the end of the seclusion policy in the middle of the nineteenth century has experienced a somewhat similar phenomenon as the Japanese have set about with great energy to translate works of Western science, literature, and philosophy and introduce them to their country. But this introduction of Western culture through translation in Japan is a process that has been going on for little more than a hundred years, hardly a fit comparison to the thousand years in which the Chinese devoted themselves to the translation of

Buddhist literature. Moreover, the methods of translation and the social conditions relating to translation work differed greatly in the case of ancient China and of Japan in the past century. To cite merely one example, the use of printing makes it possible today to produce books rapidly and in great numbers, but in the China of early times, each word of the text had to be written out by hand with a brush. Thus the production and dissemination of translations of foreign works required an enormous amount of time and labor. Perhaps only a country such as China, with a culture stretching back many centuries and a profound respect for the written word, could have mustered the energy and patience to carry out such an arduous undertaking.

At the time of the introduction of Buddhism to China, the Chinese already had a vast literature of their own dating to around 1000 B.C. or earlier. The core of this rich literary heritage was the group of works known as the *Wu-ching,* or Five Confucian Classics, texts that were either compiled by or connected in some way with the sage Confucius. These texts held the same place of importance in Confucian teaching as the sutras did in the teachings of Buddhism, as attested by the fact that the Chinese used the word *ching* or "classic" when they translated the Sanskrit word *sūtra.* The Confucian Classics were regarded as embodying all the traditional wisdom of ancient China and over the centuries were provided with extensive commentaries to make clear their meaning. In the Han period, when Confucianism was adopted as the official creed of the state and a national university was established, scholars were appointed to give instruction in each of the Five Classics.

It is natural enough, of course, that the Chinese should treat their own works of literature with profound respect, since such works represented the finest products of their native tradition. But, as we have noted before, the Chinese often tended to look down on the cultures of other countries and to be suspicious of foreign customs and ways of thought, particularly when they differed markedly from those of China. We may suppose that Buddhist ideas and writings were at first regarded with the same suspicion and attacked on the grounds of their foreign origin. In time, however, a certain number of persons began to take an interest in the new religion. It is probable, as the accounts suggest, that they looked on it merely as a kind of magical or semimagical means for securing health and long life, something akin to the practices and beliefs of religious Taoism, the cult of the Yellow Emperor and Lao Tzu. Eventually, however, they came to understand that this new religion imported from the Western Region was in fact one of the most complex and important teachings ever to appear in the course of human history. And once they had become convinced of that fact, they were impatient to see its scriptures translated into Chinese so that its doctrines might be handed down to later generations in China.

As a result of this task of translation carried out over a period of a thousand years, Buddhism came to exert a tremendous influence over the thought and development of the Chinese people. At least for the period from the introduction of Buddhism down to the end of the Northern Sung in 1126, when this translation work was being carried on, it is impossible to discuss either Chinese history or culture without taking Buddhist influence into account. Moreover, if we survey this thousand-year period during which China was most receptive to Buddhist teaching and influence, we can, by observing the different types of texts that were translated at different times during the period, surmise something about the kind of Buddhism that prevailed and the social conditions of the time. The history of Buddhist translation in China, in other words, is none other than the history of the rise, glory, and decline of Buddhism in China. Even in the broader development of Chinese culture, it is a factor of unmistakable importance during the thousand-year period when translation work was being carried on.

But let us leave these generalities for a moment and examine some of the important figures in the early part of this period of translation to see just how this process of Buddhist influence on Chinese history and culture operated.

We will look first at the figure of Chu Shih-hsing, the earliest known example of a Chinese who renounced secular life to become a member of the Buddhist priesthood. He was a native of Yingch'uan in present-day Honan Province, and was said to have been well versed in the Prajna, or Wisdom, sutras. When he happened to learn that the Prajna sutras he was familiar with did not represent the most complete exposition of that doctrine, he set out from Yung-chou in Shensi Province in A.D. 260 and journeyed west as far as the state of Khotan in Central Asia. There he obtained a copy of the twenty-five-thousand–line version of the *Prajna Sutra,* which he entrusted to the disciples accompanying him, charging them to take it back with them to China. He himself was nearly eighty by this time and destined to die in the Western Region, but the text which his disciples took back with them to China was in time translated into Chinese as the *Light-Emitting Perfection of Wisdom Sutra* in twenty volumes.

Chu Shih-hsing lived in the third century, the Three Kingdoms period, when China was divided into three rival states contending for power. Chu was a native of northern China, which at that time was under the control of the Wei dynasty. In the valley of the Yangtze River and south of it was the state of Wu, headed by a ruler named Sun Ch'üan, who became a convert to Buddhism. The person credited with the conversion was a monk named K'ang Seng-hui, who lived a stormy and eventful life.

Biographical information concerning K'ang Seng-hui and other monks of this period is found in *A Collection of Records Concerning the Tripitaka,* a work finished around 518 by the monk Seng-yu. It is the oldest extant catalogue of Chinese translations of Buddhist works and a valuable source of information on the early history of Buddhism in China. According to the *Collection of Records,* K'ang Seng-hui's ancestors were natives of the Central Asian state of Sogdiana (K'ang-chü). Later they moved to India, and from there in time made their way to Chiao-chih in the northern part of present-day Vietnam, where they engaged in business. When K'ang Seng-hui was only around ten, however, both his parents died and thereafter he became a Buddhist monk.

In 247, he took up residence in Chien-yeh, the Wu capital city on the site of modern Nanking, where he produced such translations as the *Liu-tu-chi Ching,* a work describing the six paramitas, the practices required of Mahayana bodhisattvas in order to attain

Buddhahood. He is said to have been particularly skilled at the musical chanting of sacred texts, but his main concern seems to have been the propagation and practice of the faith. In addition to converting the ruler of the state, Sun Ch'üan, to Buddhism, he was also very active in spreading a knowledge of Buddhism among the masses and founded the Chien-ch'u-ssu, the first Buddhist temple in the Yangtze valley region.

Another translator of Buddhist texts who was active in the Yangtze region was Chih Ch'ien, a lay Buddhist believer who enjoyed the patronage of Sun Ch'üan and produced translations of a number of Mahayana works. His grandfather was Chih Fa-tu, a native of Kushana who emigrated to China and settled there. Chih Ch'ien received instruction in the faith from Chih Liang, a disciple of the Kushana monk Lokaraksha, mentioned earlier, who had come to China in the Later Han dynasty.

As a result of the ardent efforts of these Buddhist believers who braved the dangers of the road and traveled to China from the second century onward, the foreign faith began to take root in Chinese soil and to spread among the population. By the time of the Three Kingdoms period, a new cultural era was dawning in the long history of the Chinese people.

We must always bear in mind that human history is not determined by political and economic factors alone. In the society of every period, stretching away in the background behind the great statesmen and other prominent figures of the time, is the vast plane of ordinary human activity, and developments among the masses working and living their lives on that plane must also be taken into consideration. The Three Kingdoms period was a time of great political and social turmoil, and it would appear that the hearts and minds of the common people were thirsty for some kind of spiritual aid. They were in a mood to be receptive to the teachings of the imported faith. We must understand this fact if we are to understand why Buddhism made such rapid advances among the people of the period. We must also take cognizance of the activities of the monk-translators and the number of persons who as a result of their labors were won over to the Buddhist faith if we are to rightly judge the basic forces that were at work in shaping the history and cultural development of the time.

During the Three Kingdoms period, the Chin dynasty (265–420) that followed it, and the period of the Northern and Southern dynasties (420–581)—that is, from the third to the sixth century—the number of temples and of monks and nuns increased dramatically, an indication of how rapidly and thoroughly Buddhism was spreading among the Chinese masses. According to records of the time, at the end of the sixth century the area of northern China boasted over thirty thousand temples and a population of monks and nuns numbering two million. In the region of the Yangtze and south, where the Liang dynasty ruled from 502 to 557, there are reported to have been over 2,800 temples and 82,700 monks and nuns. In addition, of course, there must have been great numbers of lay believers. It is apparent that Buddhism had by this time become firmly established in China.

To be sure, scholars point out that because of the troubled nature of the time many persons must have become monks or nuns simply to escape hardship and insure themselves of a living. Moreover, one important reason for the spread of Buddhism in the area of the Yangtze and south was that as a result of the invasion of barbarian armies from the north and the fall of the Chinese capitals of Lo-yang and Ch'ang-an in the early part of the fourth century many Chinese living in the north were forced to flee south, and those who had already converted to Buddhism naturally took their faith with them.

These were no doubt factors in the rapid spread of Buddhism. But I would like to think that the phenomenon was due to the powerful energy innate in Buddhism itself, which allowed it to overcome all obstacles and spread among the Chinese populace, and to the fact that it contained the kind of lofty doctrines capable of winning adherents in any land and among any people.

One manifestation of that energy was surely the staggering volume of Buddhist works that were translated into Chinese, and the volume and excellence of these translations in turn was one of the major factors accounting for the rapid dissemination of the faith and the enormous impact that it had on Chinese history and culture. The Chinese Tripitaka, or canon of Buddhist works, which is divided into the three categories of sutras, rules of discipline, and treatises, contains a total of 1,440 works running to 5,586 volumes. This huge mass of translations represents not only a crowning achievement in the history of Chinese Buddhism, but a priceless cultural legacy bequeathed to all humankind.

3. Kumarajiva and
His Translation Activities

The Unparalleled Monk-Translator

Let us turn our attention now to the most outstanding of all the translators of Buddhist texts who came to China from the Western Region, Kumarajiva, and examine his contribution to the propagation of Buddhism in China.

Nichiren Daishonin, in a letter replying to the wife of Lord Ōta (*Ōta-dono Nyōbō Gohenji*), writes: "There were 176 persons who transmitted the sutras and treatises from India to China. Among all these, Kumarajiva alone relayed the sutras and other writings of Shakyamuni, the founder, without interjecting any of his own private opinions. Of these 175 persons other than Kumarajiva, the 164 who lived before or around the same time as Kumarajiva can be understood because of the light which Kumarajiva's wisdom throws on them. But these 164 persons who lived around the time of Kumarajiva's arrival in China clearly made errors, while the 11 later persons who produced the so-called New Translations also made errors. The latter, however, were able to become somewhat more shrewd and knowing because of Kumarajiva's labors. This is not simply my own private opinion, but is stated in the work entitled *Kanzūden,* which speaks of Kumarajiva as being 'unparalleled among both his predecessors and successors.' "

We may note that the figure of 176 persons is based on records covering the period to 730, the eighteenth year of the K'ai-yüan era in the reign of the T'ang ruler Hsüan-tsung. If we extend the period under consideration to 1285, the twenty-second year of the Chih-yüan era of Khubilai Khan of the Yüan dynasty (ca. 1280–1368), then the total number of persons known to have engaged in the Chinese translations of Buddhist texts comes to 194.

Nearly all of these monk-translators who were responsible for introducing and propagating the Buddhist texts in China came from Central Asia or reached China by way of that area. Among them, Kumarajiva, as we have seen, was one of the most distinguished. He has been universally recognized first of all for the excellence of his translations. Not only did he produce works that were noted for their skill and beauty of language, but he based himself squarely upon the philosophy of the Indian scholar Nagarjuna, whose teachings represent the orthodox line of Mahayana doctrine. Thus Kumarajiva carried out a task of inestimable merit in making certain that the Buddhist teachings were correctly transmitted to the Chinese. At the same time, we should recognize that the fact that such basic Mahayana texts as the *Lotus Sutra,* the *Larger Perfection of Wisdom Sutra,* and the *Vimalakirti Sutra* came to be so widely studied and revered throughout China was due not only to the superior nature of the ideas expressed in these texts but also to the fact that Kumarajiva's translations of them are couched in such powerful and compelling language.

We should keep these points in mind when we come to assess the importance and influence of his translation endeavors. But before considering his activities as a translator, let us examine his background and period of early training to see if we can better understand the forces that led him to become one of the world's most renowned translators.

KUMARAJIVA'S PARENTAGE

Something of Kumarajiva's background and the ups and downs of his stormy life can be learned from Chinese sources such as *Biographies of Eminent Monks,* a collection of biographies of outstanding Buddhist figures in China compiled by a monk of the Liang dynasty named Hui-chiao (497–554). As in the case of lives of saints and outstanding religious figures in any country, we must of course allow for the possibility that certain events in his story may have been exaggerated or idealized by biographers writing in the years following his death.

To begin with, it is difficult to determine just exactly when he was born and died. According to the "Posthumous Eulogy for the Dharma Master Kumarajiva" written by Seng-chao (384–414), a disciple of Kumarajiva, and preserved in the collection of Buddhist texts known as the *Kuang Hung-ming Chi,* he died in 413 at the age of sixty-nine, or seventy by Chinese reckoning, which means that he was born in 344. According to his biography in *Eminent Monks,* however, he was born in 350 and died in 409, which means that he was only fifty-nine at the time of his death.

But if we are uncertain as to just exactly when he lived and how long, we are far better off than we are in the case of such famous Indian Buddhist figures as Shakyamuni, Nagarjuna, Asanga, or Vasubandhu, where scholars differ by as much as one or two centuries in estimating the period when they lived. This is due, needless to say, to the fact that the Chinese have always taken far more interest in the keeping of historical records than have the Indians. If Kumarajiva had not journeyed from Central Asia and spent his last years in China, we might not even know that he existed.

But to return to the subject of his biography. According to *Eminent Monks,* he was of Indian descent on his father's side. His father came from a distinguished family that for some generations had served as prime ministers to an Indian kingdom. Kumarajiva's father, Kumarayana, likewise had been promised the post of prime minister, but because he did not see eye to eye with the ruler of the kingdom, he renounced his right to the position and became a Buddhist monk instead. Thereafter he set out on a journey eastward that took him over the Pamir Mountains to Central Asia.

We do not know for certain just what motives led Kumarayana to embark on such a journey, though it was probably more than mere political disappointment that impelled him to turn his back on his native land. Perhaps he felt a sense of religious mission, realizing that the Buddhist teachings were not meant for the people of India alone and hoping to bring enlightenment and blessing to the peoples of other countries by working to spread them in the regions of Central Asia and beyond.

We may perhaps envision him setting out on his journey with a wooden image of Shakyamuni Buddha strapped to his back, making his way over the difficult passes of the Hindu Kush until he emerged on the plateaus of the Pamirs, and from there pushing eastward through the shifting sands of the Taklamakan Desert. Given the primitive conditions of travel that prevailed at the time, it must have been an exceedingly difficult journey. Taking the route that led along the northern border of the desert, he came in time to the small state of Kucha on the northern edge of the Tarim Basin. According to accounts, the ruler of the state, learning of his arrival, went out in person to the suburbs of the capital to greet him, treating him with the honor due a highly distinguished guest.

As noted earlier, the region of Central Asia had by this time already been converted to Buddhism, and Kucha was among the most fervently Buddhist states in the area. Kumarayana was probably aware of this fact, and if he had determined to quit his native land for religious reasons, it would seem likely that he intended to pass through Kucha and continue on his way as far as China in order to help propagate the faith there.

The king of Kucha, however, had other plans for Kumarayana. Recognizing his ability and eminence, the king hoped to persuade him to remain in Kucha and serve as a Teacher of the Nation. At this time, persons honored with the title of Teacher of the Nation, while serving as leaders of the Buddhist faith, also functioned as cultural and political advisors and planners. In view of the complicated and ever-shifting diplomatic relations among the numerous small states of Central Asia, it was of great importance to the ruler to have competent people to act as his counselors in such matters.

For this reason, the king of Kucha treated Kumarayana with great favor, going so far as to offer him his own younger sister as a bride. According to the biography of Kumarajiva in the *Collection of Records Concerning the Tripitaka,* the proffered bride was around twenty years of age, a woman "of great talent and perspicacity, who had only to glance over a written passage to master it, had only to hear something one time to be able to repeat it from memory." She had earlier been the recipient of numerous offers of marriage from the neighboring states of Central Asia, but had rejected them all. As soon as she laid eyes on Kumarayana, however, her heart was moved, we are told, and she expressed her desire to become his wife.

"When the king heard this," the biography informs us, "he was overjoyed and pressed Kumarayana to take the girl for his bride, and from their union Kumarajiva in time was born." The bride's name was Jivaka, and when her son was born, the element Kumara, taken from his father's name, was combined with the element Jiva from his mother's name to form the name Kumarajiva. Kumarajiva was thus the offspring of an international marriage and brought up in a state that played an important role in cultural exchanges between eastern and western Asia.

Kumarayana, of course, had already taken religious vows and become a monk before he reached the state of Kucha, and it must have been deeply troubling for him to have to transgress the rules of the Order, which forbade marriage, and take a wife. Interestingly, his son Kumarajiva was in time to face the same dilemma. The fact that both father and son were destined to undergo this disquieting experience no doubt did much to deepen their sympathy and understanding of human nature. I would surmise that it was one of the reasons why Kumarajiva gave his allegiance to the Mahayana teachings rather than to those of Hinayana Buddhism. While the Hinayana teachings enjoin the monk to hold himself aloof from society and devote himself to his own spiritual cultivation, the bodhisattva ideal held up by the Mahayana envisions a more active life, one that vigorously challenges the ills of society and labors for the salvation of all humankind.

THE PERIOD OF YOUTHFUL STUDY

Kumarajiva's biographers describe him as a child of remarkable genius. At the age of seven (six by Western reckoning), he left secular life and entered the Buddhist Order. His mother at the same time became a Buddhist nun. He is said to have memorized a thousand verses of the sutras, the equivalent of thirty-two thousand words, each day. By the time he had memorized the entire Abhidharma, the division of the Buddhist canon consisting of doctrinal commentaries, he could comprehend everything that his teacher said to him and perceive its hidden meaning.

When he was nine years old his mother, thinking to broaden the scope of his religious training, set out with him on a journey to India, crossing the Indus River and entering the state known in Chinese as Chi-pin in the area of present-day Kashmir. This was the region from which his father had come.

There Kumarajiva studied under an eminent Buddhist master named Bandhudatta, who was a cousin of the ruler of the country. Under him, Kumarajiva is said to have mastered the various Hinayana sutras known as the Agamas in the northern tradition of Buddhism and the Nikayas in the southern tradition. It is also said that, despite his great youth, he prevailed in debate over teachers of non-Buddhist doctrines in the presence of the ruler of Chi-pin. The ruler, deeply impressed, assigned five full-fledged monks and ten novices to him as his disciples and otherwise treated him with the greatest respect. It was no doubt around this time that his reputation began to spread throughout India and the states of Central Asia.

At the age of twelve, Kumarajiva and his mother set out for the return journey to Kucha. According to his biography in *Eminent Monks,* the rulers of the various states in the region, having heard of his fame, "all presented him with imposing titles." Kumarajiva, however, refused to accept any such honors and proceeded with his mother to the territory of the Yüeh-chih people. On their way back to Kucha, Kumarajiva passed through the northern mountains in the Yüeh-chih territory and there encountered an arhat, or Buddhist saint, who made a strange prediction concerning his future. Because of the light it throws on the destiny that lay in store for him, his biographers have taken care to record the prophecy. Speaking to Kumarajiva's mother, the arhat said: "You must watch over and protect this novice. If by the time he reaches the age of thirty-five he has not broken any of the rules of religious discipline, he will become a great propagator of the Buddhist teachings, bringing enlightenment to countless persons, and will be the equal of Upagupta. But if he is unable to keep the rules of religious discipline, then he will be nothing more than a highly talented and distinguished Dharma Master."

Upagupta, who is mentioned in the prophecy, was the third, or according to some reckonings, the fourth of the Indian patriarchs of Buddhism and a highly distinguished monk who is famous for converting King Ashoka to the faith. Looking ahead in the story of Kumarajiva's life, we may note that he did in fact eventually break the rules of monastic discipline, but in spite of that he became a great propagator of the Buddhist teachings, as the arhat had predicted.

Leaving the region of the Yüeh-chih, Kumarajiva and his mother proceeded to the state of Kashgar, where they stayed for a year. During this period, his biography tells us, he completed his studies of Hinayana works such as the Abhidharma texts and the writings of the Sarvastivada school.

In addition to his studies of Buddhist works, Kumarajiva at this time also turned his attention to non-Buddhist texts such as the Vedic literature, the religious and philosophical works of ancient India. He also studied texts on specialized subjects such as medicine, astronomy, exegetics, technology, and logic, as well as the systems of chanting associated with the Vedas. In other words, he acquired a wide knowledge of the arts and sciences as they were

known to the world of India and Central Asia at that time. This
knowledge was to assist him greatly in his later activities as a translator, particularly when he came to translate such encyclopedic
texts as the *Treatise on the Larger Perfection of Wisdom.* Without this
background he might never have been able to comprehend such
texts, much less render them intelligibly into Chinese.

During this period, when he was acquiring the broad foundation
of knowledge that would support him in his later activities, he was
no doubt perfecting his linguistic ability as well, gaining a mastery
of Sanskrit and Pali, the languages of the Buddhist canon, as well
as of the various languages of Central Asia.

While he was resident in the country, Kumarajiva was invited
to ascend the seat of honor and to expound to the assembly the
Sutra of the Turning of the Wheel of the Law. For a monk of his young
age to be accorded such honor at a religious assembly was surely
most extraordinary, and the people of Kashgar must have been
deeply impressed by the profound learning and mastery of languages that he displayed. According to the description of the event
in *Eminent Monks,* it would appear that the ruler himself attended
the assembly to hear Kumarajiva's preaching of the Law.

The idea of holding this religious assembly and inviting Kumarajiva to preach at it was suggested to the ruler by one of the
eminent monks of the kingdom, who advised the ruler to treat
Kumarajiva, young as he was, with all respect. He predicted that
two benefits would derive from such an assembly. First, the monks
of Kashgar, when they observed how superior Kumarajiva was in
his learning and understanding, would be shamed into greater
efforts to improve their own understanding. Second, when the
ruler of Kumarajiva's own state of Kucha observed the great respect that was paid to Kumarajiva by the ruler of Kashgar, he
would be moved to enter into friendly intercourse with the kingdom. This, in fact, is exactly what happened, the ruler of Kucha
dispatching a party of high-ranking ministers to Kashgar for that
purpose. Thus this young monk was instrumental in establishing
harmonious relations between these two oasis kingdoms of the
Central Asian desert.

Another important event in Kumarajiva's life that took place at this time was his meeting with the monk Sutyasoma. Sutyasoma was a prince of the state of Yarkand, or So-ch'e, another oasis kingdom in the Tarim Basin. Both Sutyasoma and his older brother, Sutyabadda, had left secular life and become monks and were residing in Kashgar in order to undergo religious training. Sutyasoma, the younger brother, was a follower of the Mahayana teachings and worked to spread them among the populace. Both his older brother and a number of other monks, according to the account in *Eminent Monks,* looked up to him as their teacher.

We can only surmise just how Kumarajiva came to become acquainted with Sutyasoma. Perhaps the latter attended Kumarajiva's expositions of the Law and, while admiring the young monk's great breadth of learning, felt a certain inadequacy in their content, since they were based upon Hinayana doctrines. Perhaps some of Sutyasoma's own disciples approached Kumarajiva and pointed out to him the limitations of the Hinayana interpretation of the Buddha's teaching. Or perhaps Kumarajiva himself, having exhausted the study of the Hinayana sutras and the treatises of the Sarvastivada school, which hold that the dharmas, or elements of phenomenal existence, are ultimately real, felt the need to delve deeper into Buddhist philosophy. If so, he may have taken the initiative in approaching Sutyasoma and asking for instruction. In view of his own youthful age, it would have been only natural for him to take such a step as a gesture of respect for the senior monk.

In any event, according to *Eminent Monks,* Sutyasoma expounded for Kumarajiva the *Anuttara Sutra,* which teaches that all dharmas are "empty," or lacking in definable characteristics. Kumarajiva was unable to comprehend this doctrine of the Mahayana and, frankly expressing his doubt and confusion, asked, "What doctrine is this sutra expounding? Why does it preach the destruction of all the elements of existence?"

To this Sutyasoma replied, "The elements of existence are based upon the evidence of the eyes and the other senses and do not have any real existence." In other words, since all the elements of existence are the product of causation and dependent origination, they cannot be properly comprehended on the basis of the evidence given to us by the eyes and the other senses. This statement by Sutyasoma served to awaken Kumarajiva to the profundity of the Mahayana teachings, and thereafter he immersed himself in study in order to determine just how the Mahayana doctrines differed from those of the Hinayana. Looking back on his earlier beliefs, he is said to have reported with a sigh that, while he was studying the Hinayana doctrines, he was like a person who doesn't know what gold is and mistakes mere brass for something wonderful.

Pursuing his study of the Mahayana teachings, he received instruction in the *Treatise on the Middle Way* (Ch., *Chung Lun;* J., *Chu Ron*) and the *Treatise on the Twelve Gates* (Ch., *Shih-erh Men Lun;* J., *Juni Mon Ron*) of the Indian philosopher Nagarjuna and the *Treatise in One Hundred Verses* (Ch., *Pai [Po] Lun;* J., *Hyaku Ron*) of Aryadeva, memorizing these important texts of Mahayana philosophy.

This encounter with Sutyasoma marked a crucial turning point in Kumarajiva's life, reminding us of how important it is to come in contact with a truly outstanding teacher. Many years later, after Kumarajiva had journeyed to China and had completed his translation of the *Lotus Sutra,* he is reported to have spoken the following memorable words to his disciples. "In the past, when I was in India, I traveled around to all the five lands of India seeking the teachings of the Mahayana. When I came to study under Great Teacher Sutyasoma, I was able to savor the taste of true understanding. He entrusted his Sanskrit texts to me and charged me with the propagation of the sutras, saying, 'The sun of the Buddha has gone into hiding behind the western mountains, but its lingering rays shine over the northeast. These texts are destined for the lands of the northeast. You must make certain that they are transmitted to them!' "

After his year of study in Kashgar, Kumarajiva and his mother left the state and, after stopping for a time in Wen-su, another oasis kingdom in the vicinity, returned to Kucha. By this time Kumarajiva's fame had spread as far as China, and numerous monks flocked to him from many different countries to receive instruction. As a teacher of Mahayana Buddhism, he had no rival in India, Central Asia, or China, and he was fully prepared now to set off for China to carry out his missionary activities there. But a number of years were to pass before he could realize his hopes, years that were beset by numerous difficulties and vicissitudes of fortune.

THE ROAD TO CH'ANG-AN

Kumarajiva entered Ch'ang-an on the twentieth day of the twelfth month of the third year of the Hung-shih era of the Later Ch'in dynasty, a date that would actually fall early in 402 by the Western calendar, though it is usually given as 401 because the third year of the Hung-shih era corresponds for the most part with 401. According to the account of his life in the *Kuang Hung-ming Chi,* he was fifty-seven at the time, though his biography in *Eminent Monks* gives his age as fifty-one. Recent studies seem to favor the latter assertion.

At fifty, Confucius is said to have "understood the will of Heaven." In a sense, the fifties are the period when a person puts the finishing touches on his or her life. The creativity of the individual customarily makes its appearance in the person's twenties or thirties, while the forties witness the growth and development of these earlier creative impulses. In one's fifties, one brings the process of development to fulfillment.

Certainly for Kumarajiva, the fifties, after his entry into Ch'ang-an, represented the most fruitful period of his life, when his powers reached their highest level of development. But this bright period of fulfillment was preceded by many long years of hardship and frustration.

After his year of study in Kashgar, Kumarajiva and his mother returned to their home in Kucha. There at the age of twenty Kumarajiva ended his long period as a *shramanera,* or novice, and received the rites of ordination that made him a full-fledged monk in the Buddhist Order. Sometime later his mother, distressed by the declining fortunes of the state of Kucha, took leave of her son and set off on a journey for India. She no doubt realized that she would never see him again, and at the time of parting, according to *Eminent Monks,* urged him to work to spread the profound teachings of the Mahayana doctrine in China. He alone, she counseled, was capable of carrying out this task, though he must expect no personal gain from the endeavor.

Kumarajiva, we are told, replied that the ideal of the Mahayana bodhisattva demanded that one set aside all considerations of personal gain or safety and work to bring benefit to others. If he could spread the Mahayana teachings throughout China, dispelling darkness and ignorance and making people aware of the inferior nature of the Hinayana doctrines, then even though he might be tortured with burning irons, he would have no regrets. In view of the manner in which events were to develop, it is well that Kumarajiva faced the future with this degree of zeal and resignation.

Kumarajiva was around thirty-two (or, according to the *Collection of Records Concerning the Tripitaka,* thirty-three) when he first set foot on Chinese soil. It came about because he was taken prisoner by a military leader and forcibly brought to China.

China at this time was in a period of internal division and political instability. Northern China was ruled by a series of short-lived dynasties founded by non-Chinese invaders, many of whom patronized the Buddhist religion. One of the most important of these leaders was Fu Chien (338–85), the forceful third ruler of a dynasty known as the Former Ch'in, who for a time exercised control over all of northern China. It was he who set in motion the steps that were to bring Kumarajiva to China.

Earlier, in 379, Fu Chien, having consolidated his control over northern China, dispatched armies to attack and capture the city of Hsiang-yang in Hupei, where the eminent Buddhist monk Tao-an (314–85) was residing. He persuaded Tao-an, along with his literary friend Hsi Tso-ch'ih, to come to Ch'ang-an, where Fu Chien had his capital. There Tao-an took up residence in a temple called the Wu-chung-ssu and spent the remaining years of his life giving religious instruction to several thousand disciples and overseeing the translation of Buddhist works into Chinese. The monks whom he trained and supervised in these activities were later to be extremely helpful to Kumarajiva in his own translation activities in Ch'ang-an. In this sense, Tao-an served to lay the foundation for Kumarajiva's endeavors.

Tao-an, having heard of Kumarajiva's fame, suggested that the latter might be persuaded to come to Ch'ang-an. Fu Chien, pleased with the suggestion, set about putting it into effect in his customary forceful manner by dispatching a military leader named Lü Kuang to march to the west and attack the state of Kucha, where Kumarajiva was living. This took place in 382 or 383. Having overthrown Kucha and taken Kumarajiva prisoner, Lü Kuang was on his way back to China when he received word that Fu Chien had been taken prisoner and killed by a leader of the Yao family, who proceeded to set up a new dynasty known as the Later Ch'in. Lü Kuang thereupon declared himself an independent ruler in the Liang-chou region of present-day Kansu, setting up a state known as the Later Liang. Kumarajiva was held in captivity at Ku-tsang, the capital of the state, and remained there for sixteen years.

Just what kind of life Kumarajiva led during these sixteen years is not made clear in the accounts of his career, so we must go largely on conjecture. It would appear that he acted as a military adviser to Lü Kuang. Lü Kuang seems to have been a man of rather mean character. When he followed Kumarajiva's advice, he achieved a certain measure of success, but more often he ignored it, and was several times forced to face rebellion among his subordinates. In addition, he had no understanding or appreciation of Buddhism and subjected Kumarajiva to various indignities, plying him with wine, forcing him to have sexual relations with a princess of the state of Kucha, or ordering him to ride oxen or evil-tempered horses in hopes of seeing him fall off. These eighteen years in the Liang-chou border region were no doubt a period of great trial and hardship for Kumarajiva, and that is probably why his disciples, when they came to compile accounts of his life, preferred to say as little about the period as possible.

During his years in Liang-chou, Kumarajiva must have devoted himself to study of the Chinese language and gained considerable fluency in it. Though it is no more than conjecture, I like to think of him as gazing far off at the eastern sky, longing to make his way to Ch'ang-an, the ancient center of traditional Chinese culture, where he could carry out his mission to transmit the orthodox line of Mahayana teachings to the Chinese people. Since it gave him an opportunity to acquire an invaluable command of the Chinese language, his period of detention in Liang-chou was not a total loss. Like so many great men, Kumarajiva through his efforts turned what otherwise would have been a period of loss into one of gain.

The period was also important, I think, because it gave him a chance to mingle with the rough soldiers and other inhabitants of the border region and to see something of the lower side of Chinese life. Most of the monk-translators who had come to China in the past had been men of highly distinguished position who were welcomed by the rulers and aristocracy of China or the members of the intellectual class, and unlike Kumarajiva had little opportunity to become acquainted with life on other levels of Chinese society. They mingled with and addressed themselves almost exclusively to the upper classes rather than trying to spread their message among the masses, which may be one reason why no clear distinction had yet been made between the Hinayana and the Mahayana teachings in the doctrines they transmitted.

The Yao family, rulers of the Later Ch'in dynasty with their capital in Ch'ang-an, had made repeated efforts to bring Kumarajiva to Ch'ang-an, but Lü Kuang refused to release him. Finally Yao Hsing (366–416), the second ruler of the Later Ch'in, sent his armies west to attack and overthrow Lü Kuang's state and bring Kumarajiva back with them to Ch'ang-an.

Thus, probably in the fall of 401, Kumarajiva was at last able to turn his back on Ku-tsang, the desert outpost that had served as Lü Kuang's base of operation, and make his way to Ch'ang-an. As we have seen, he entered the city, warmly welcomed by the rulers there, near the end of the twelfth lunar month of the Chinese year, as winter was coming to a close. His disciples no doubt took care to record the exact month and day of his entry because they realized that it marked a momentous date in the history of Chinese Buddhism.

THE NATURE OF KUMARAJIVA'S TRANSLATIONS

As soon as Kumarajiva had entered Ch'ang-an, he responded to the wishes of the ruler by setting to work immediately on the translation of Buddhist texts. At the request of a Chinese monk named Seng-jui, who was to become one of his most important disciples, he commenced work on the twenty-sixth day of the month, only six days after his arrival, translating a text on meditation practices entitled *Tso-ch'an San-mei Ching*. In the following year, 402, he began work on the hundred-volume *Treatise on the Larger Perfection of Wisdom*, which seems to have progressed with great rapidity. One can only be amazed at the speed and smoothness with which his translation activities proceeded.

Counting both retranslations and works translated for the first time, Kumarajiva is said to have translated over fifty works, running to more than three hundred volumes. The *Collection of Records* gives the somewhat smaller figures of thirty-five works in 294 volumes, but whichever set of figures we accept, the amount is impressive. If we follow *Eminent Monks* in regarding 409 as the year of his death, during his eight years of residence in Ch'ang-an he must have translated at the rate of approximately one chapter every ten days. And even if we accept 413, the date put forward by the *Kuang Hung-ming Chi* as the year of his demise, which would give him twelve years of residence in Ch'ang-an, he would still have had to translate over two chapters a month in order to complete the volume of translations attributed to him. The fact that he pressed ahead with such assiduity is an indication of just how great was the demand in China at the time for reliable translations of Buddhist works.

The earlier translations of Buddhist texts had nearly all been done by foreign monks from the states of Central Asia. Though their translations were faithful enough to the original texts, they were often difficult for Chinese readers to comprehend. In the rare cases where the translators had strained to make the sense more easily comprehensible in Chinese, they had usually departed from or distorted the basic meaning of the texts. The Chinese had apparently experienced particular difficulty in fathoming the numerous texts dealing with the Mahayana concept of prajna, or Supreme Wisdom. The fact that Kumarajiva set out so expeditiously to translate the *Treatise on the Larger Perfection of Wisdom,* which is a commentary on one of the most important of the sutras expounding this doctrine, is no doubt an indication of how eager the Chinese Buddhist world at the time was to gain a greater understanding of it. It is said that Tao-an's leading disciples, as well as the monk Seng-jui mentioned above, rejoiced that after attending the sessions in which Kumarajiva produced his translations, they were for the first time able to comprehend the concept of *shunyata,* or emptiness, that lies at the core of the Prajna literature.

One of the main reasons Kumarajiva could proceed so rapidly with his translation work was no doubt the fact that, during his long years of study in India and the states of Central Asia, he had committed to memory nearly all the important works of Buddhism. And of course he not only had memorized the words of the text, but had acquired a thorough grasp of the profound philosophical concepts underlying them. It would not be too much to say that he had the entire Buddhist canon at his fingertips. That is why, when he took the texts in hand and set about expounding them in Chinese, his explanations could be taken down by scribes and immediately shaped into translations of the texts.

According to descriptions left by his disciples, this in fact is the way in which the translations were produced. One of these disciples, Hui-kuan, in his introduction to the *Fa-hua Tsung-yao,* writes: "Kumarajiva would take the foreign sutra in hand and would translate it orally into the language of China. He would explain it thoroughly in Chinese and at the same time would never violate the meaning of the original." Similarly, Seng-jui's introduction to the translation of the *Larger Perfection of Wisdom Sutra* states: "The master would take the foreign text in his hand and would expound it orally in the language of China. In addition, he transcribed the foreign sounds and from time to time explained the meaning of the text."

We are also told that Yao Hsing would on occasion attend the translation sessions. "The Ch'in ruler in person would hold the text of the older translations of the sutras in his hand, check them for errors, inquire about the general purport of the passage, and thus make clear the doctrines of the sect." The sessions would be attended by over five hundred scholar-monks who, after making certain that Kumarajiva's translation of the particular passage was superior to that of the older translation, would then take up their writing brushes and record it. The whole process, therefore, was a corporate undertaking that was carried out under government sponsorship.

The Japanese Buddhist scholar Enichi Ocho has pointed out four factors that were of prime importance in the production of these superb translations by Kumarajiva. First, he was a man of outstanding linguistic talent who possessed a command of Sanskrit, the languages of Central Asia, and Chinese. Second, he had a broad understanding of all phases of Buddhist doctrine, having mastered not only the Hinayana Sarvastivada writings but the Mahayana works dealing with the concept of prajna and the Madhyamika teachings, and he was conversant with the vinaya, or rules of monastic discipline, as well. Third is the fact that Yao Hsing and the leaders of the Chinese Buddhist world of the time took steps to create conditions that would be ideal for the production of Kumarajiva's translations. Fourth and finally, Kumarajiva had many talented young disciples and assistants to aid him in his labors.

The Translation of the *Lotus Sutra*

As we have seen, though Kumarajiva himself was born in the Central Asian state of Kucha, his father was a native of India, and he himself was able in his youth to travel to India and spend some

time in study there, acquiring a knowledge of Sanskrit and studying the doctrines of Buddhism in the land of their origin. It was
this solid linguistic foundation along with his innate talent and
brilliance that enabled him to become renowned among the states
of Central Asia. In addition, he spent sixteen long years as a
virtual prisoner in Liang-chou on the far western border of China.
Though his associates were probably mainly rough soldiers of the
type that inhabited the frontier regions, he was able in their company to acquire a command of spoken Chinese. It is probable that
he also learned to read and write the language as well.

To assist him in learning to read Chinese, he may well have
studied the Chinese translations of Buddhist texts that had been
made in the preceding centuries. If he did so, he would in time
have become aware of how clumsy these translations were and how
often they distorted the teachings of Buddhism or presented them
in mistaken form. Let us look, for example, at the earlier translation of the *Lotus Sutra* made in 286 by the monk Chu Fa-hu and
entitled *Cheng Fa-hua Ching*. Chu Fa-hu was a man of great linguistic talent and was said to have a command of all the languages of
Central Asia. But even he, when he translated the *Lotus Sutra* into
Chinese, had to rely heavily on the help of two assistant translators.
He apparently did not have sufficient understanding of Chinese
syntax to translate the text himself.

But it is not merely the lack of skill in the handling of language
that distinguishes Chu Fa-hu's early translation of the *Lotus Sutra*
from the translation made in 406, 120 years later, by Kumarajiva.
Unless one has a sound understanding of the doctrines expounded
in the text—and we touch here on the second of the four factors
mentioned above that contributed to Kumarajiva's outstanding
achievement as a translator—one is constantly in danger of mis-
representing the ideas of the original. Even persons speaking in the
same language may express themselves so ambiguously that their
meaning is wholly misunderstood, and when one is translating into
a completely different language, the possibilities for such confusion
and misapprehension are greatly multiplied. The importance of
Kumarajiva lies in the fact that he had sufficient learning and

understanding to avoid making the kind of errors that the earlier translators had and could point out and correct such errors when they came to his attention.

We may note here that one of the reasons why Chu Fa-hu's translation of the *Lotus Sutra* differs from the later translation by Kumarajiva is the fact that the two translators translated from somewhat different versions of the text. In 601, in the Sui dynasty, a translation of the *Lotus Sutra* entitled *T'ien-p'in Miao-fa Lien-hua Ching* by the monks Jnanagupta and Dharmagupta was completed. The introduction to this translation discusses earlier translations of the *Lotus Sutra:* "Long ago, in the time of Emperor Wu of the Chin dynasty, Chu Fa-hu, a monk of Tun-huang, made a translation entitled *Cheng Fa-hua.* At the request of Yao Hsing of the Later Ch'in dynasty, Kumarajiva produced a second translation entitled *Miao-fa Lien-hua.* If we compare the two versions, we find that they are definitely not made from the same text. The version by Chu Fa-hu resembles the *tala* leaves [of India], while that by Kumarajiva resembles the writings of Kucha. Having examined the original sutras and looked carefully at these two versions, I find that the one which resembles the *tala* leaves in fact tallies with the Correct Law, while the one which resembles the writings of Kucha accords with the Mystic Law." From this it is obvious that in the seventh century, when this passage was written, the two different texts of the sutra from which the different translations had been made were still in existence.

But the most crucial difference between the two translations of the *Lotus Sutra* is the degree to which the two translators understood the doctrines underlying the text. One cannot help feeling that Kumarajiva's superior degree of understanding is closely related to his general attitude toward translation. For example, when there was some point about Buddhism that he did not fully comprehend, he did not hesitate to set aside his pride and ask for assistance from others who were more versed in the field in question. He no doubt had complete confidence in his understanding of the Mahayana doctrine of prajna and the Madhyamika teachings, which represent the legacy of Nagarjuna's scholarship. But he seems to have felt somewhat insecure in his grasp of the rules of monastic discipline. Thus, for example, he approached Yao Hsing to request that the ruler invite the Indian Buddhist scholar-monk Buddhayashas, who at this time was residing in Ku-tsang on the western border, to come to Ch'ang-an. "Though I am thoroughly conversant with the texts," Kumarajiva explained to the king, "I cannot fully comprehend the meaning. But Buddhayashas has a profound understanding of the sacred texts, and he is now in Ku-tsang. I beg that you will send an order to have him summoned, so that each word of the text can be subjected to thorough explication. After that, his views can be written down, taking care not to overlook the slightest comment, and can be relied upon for a thousand years to come." Kumarajiva did not spare any efforts in making certain that he could propagate the Buddhist teachings correctly. It is for this reason that he was able to produce so many fine translations which, as in the case of his translation of the *Lotus Sutra,* continue to be used today.

Further evidence of Kumarajiva's great learning and understanding may be found in the correspondence which he carried on with the eminent Chinese monk Hui-yüan (334–416), who at this time was living at Mount Lu in southern China. Hui-yüan wrote a series of eighteen letters to Kumarajiva questioning him on points of doctrine. These letters, along with Kumarajiva's answers, have been collected in a work entitled *Chapter on the Grand Meaning of the Mahayana*. To each query that Hui-yüan poses, Kumarajiva responds with a careful and exhaustive explanation. Through Kumarajiva's guidance the Buddhists of China were for the first time fully able to appreciate how superior the Mahayana teachings are to those of the Hinayana.

The third factor, the assistance given to Kumarajiva by the ruler of the Later Ch'in, was of utmost importance in allowing Kumarajiva to devote himself wholeheartedly to his translation activities. We should keep in mind that during this era of strife and political instability in China, Buddhist monks and believers had on numerous occasions suffered persecution and even death. Chu Fa-hu had been forced to move from place to place in order to escape becoming embroiled in conflict, leaving Tun-huang and moving about to Ch'ang-an, Lo-yang, and Chiu-ch'üan, carrying his scrolls of sacred texts on his back and conducting his translation activities as best he could. His biography in the *Collection of Records* states that "while he was journeying from Tun-huang to Ch'ang-an, he worked at the translation along the way, writing it out in Chinese."

Kumarajiva in this respect was much more fortunate in the conditions under which he worked. He too, however, had had his sixteen long years of hardship in Liang-chou before coming to Ch'ang-an. In the end it was his own years of study and application, along with his inborn talent and his profound grasp of the Mahayana teachings, that allowed him to produce such outstanding translations. The ruler's assistance simply provided him with conditions under which he could make the best possible use of his background and understanding.

And, as noted earlier, the assistance given him by his many distinguished disciples was another factor that contributed greatly to his success. We are told that when he translated the *Larger Perfection of Wisdom Sutra* over five hundred monks took part in the sessions, and at other times he had as many as two or three thousand monks attending the sessions and listening to his explanations. We may ask how there came to be such a large assembly of monk-scholars to attend Kumarajiva in his undertakings. First, we know that many talented monks from all over the country flocked to Ch'ang-an when they heard that Kumarajiva was in residence there, for he was already famous in Buddhist circles. It is also possible that the ruler of the Later Ch'in may have taken steps to encourage the assembling of such monk-scholars, or that Kumarajiva himself may have done so. And when the translations were completed, the monks who had attended the sessions then took copies of the new translations with them to other parts of the country and set about propagating the Mahayana teachings there. This last point is of particular importance, since no matter how fine a translation may be, it can never be of great effectiveness unless there are people to read it and spread its message among the populace. Hui-kuan's introduction to the *Fa-hua Tsung-yao* (mentioned earlier) as well as Seng-jui's *Later Introduction to the Lotus Sutra* make clear that anywhere from eight hundred to two thousand monks attended the sessions in which the *Lotus Sutra* was translated. When Kumarajiva's translation, the *Miao-fa Lien-hua Ching*, was completed, they were beside themselves with joy and hastened to return to their respective regions to begin the task of propagating the new translation.

Hui-kuan's introduction states: "In the summer of the eighth year of the Hung-shih era (406) of the Later Ch'in, over two thousand monks from all four directions gathered in one of the great temples of Ch'ang-an. There a new translation of this sutra [the *Lotus Sutra*] was produced, and all the members of the assembly joined in examining it and going over it thoroughly." The introduction goes on to say: "Kumarajiva spoke in clear words that contained deep principles within them; he cited examples close at hand but his meaning was far-reaching. He explained what was hidden beneath the surface of the text, and endeavored to bring out the basic ideas underlying it." Kumarajiva not only produced a Chinese translation of the text in the presence of the assembly, but explained his reasons for translating as he did and went on to lecture on the profound doctrines expounded in the text. We may imagine him listening to questions from the distinguished monks in the assembly and continuing to expand his explanations until all members of the group were satisfied. We are told by Seng-jui and others that "the members of the group, on receiving the new translation, were filled with delight, feeling as though they were standing on the summits of the Kunlun Mountains on a clear day and gazing down at the world below."

In addition to the works already mentioned, Kumarajiva also produced translations of the *Smaller Perfection of Wisdom Sutra, Diamond Sutra, Sutra on the Ten Stages, Vimalakirti Sutra, Shuramgama Sutra*, and a number of other texts. He also translated important treatises on Mahayana philosophy such as the *Treatise on the Larger Perfection of Wisdom* (Ch., *Ta-chih-tu Lun;* J., *Daichido Ron*), *Treatise on the Ten Stages, Treatise on the Middle, Treatise in One Hundred Verses,* and *Treatise on the Twelve Gates*. Through these innumerable important translations, he exercised an enormous influence upon later Chinese Buddhism and upon the Buddhism of Japan as well.

Yao Hsing, Kumarajiva's patron, was himself an avid student of Buddhism and spared no effort in encouraging and aiding Kumarajiva's translation efforts. He expressed great concern, however, that a man of Kumarajiva's enormous talent and understanding should pass away without leaving any posterity, and in time he forced Kumarajiva to move out of his monk's quarters and take up residence with a group of female attendants. This violation of monastic discipline appears to have weighed heavily on Kumarajiva's conscience. When lecturing to his disciples, we are told, he would compare himself to a lotus flower growing up out of the mud, cautioning them to heed only the lotus and have nothing to do with the mud.

When Kumarajiva was on his deathbed and taking leave of his disciples, he is reported to have said: "In my ignorance I have perhaps committed errors in the course of my translations. . . . But if there has been no error in the translations I have made, then when my body is cremated, my tongue will not be consumed by the flames." According to his biography in *Eminent Monks*, after Kumarajiva's corpse had been cremated on a funeral pyre erected in the Hsiao-yao Garden, where the translation sessions were held, his tongue was found unaltered by the flames. To a person committed to rational ways of thought, this story may be rather difficult to accept, yet Kumarajiva's disciples claimed to have witnessed the event and took care to record it as proof to later ages that Kumarajiva's numerous translations of the sacred texts were free from error.

Whatever we may think of the story of the tongue, there is no doubt that Kumarajiva's translations mark a pinnacle in the history of the Chinese translation of Buddhist works and continue to shine with undimmed luster even today. In particular, his translation of the *Lotus Sutra*, a work which represents the highest expression of the Buddhist teachings, has over the millennium and a half since its appearance been read and admired by more people than any other translation of the sutra. The story of the tongue that survived the flames may be taken as symbolic of his achievement. Though Kumarajiva himself passed away many centuries ago, his translation of the *Lotus Sutra* remains an imperishable treasure to be passed down through the ages.

4. Efforts to Systematize
the Teachings

The *Ko-i* Method and Its Limitations

Kumarajiva's entry into Ch'ang-an in 402 marked the start of a new era in the development of Chinese Buddhism. In this chapter I would like to examine the events of the succeeding one hundred years or more, when Kumarajiva's disciples were striving to bring greater clarity and systematization to the Buddhist teachings. The period comes to a close with the appearance on the scene of Chih-i, the Great Master Tien-t'ai, foremost of all the systematizers, whose life will be the subject of a succeeding chapter.

There are various views as to how the history of Chinese Buddhism ought to be divided into periods. One of the most common methods of periodization, which I would like to introduce here, is that put forward by the Japanese scholar Kogaku Fuse. This theory divides the history of Chinese Buddhism into five periods, of which the first is called the *ko-i* period. This period extends from the introduction of Buddhism to China in the Han dynasty through the time of the Three Kingdoms and up through the Chin dynasty, corresponding to the four hundred years from the beginning of the Christian era up to the time of Kumarajiva's entry into Ch'ang-an in 402.

During this initial period, it became common for expounders of the Buddhist teachings to borrow terms from the traditional Chinese writings of Confucianism and Taoism and use these familiar terms when attempting to explain Buddhist terms that were thought to be similar in meaning. This method of explication is known as *ko-i,* or "matching the meaning," and it is from this practice that the period takes its name.

It was probably inevitable that such a method of explanation should have been employed in the early years of Chinese Buddhism. China already had a long cultural history and a voluminous philosophical literature at the time of the introduction of Buddhism, and the ways of thought typical of ancient China were in many respects quite different from those represented by Buddhism. It is only natural, therefore, that the Chinese should initially have encountered considerable difficulty in grasping the teachings of the Indian religion.

Since Buddhism deals with fundamental truths concerning human life that are of universal validity, its doctrines were of course as applicable to the Chinese and other peoples of the world as they were to the people of the country where it originated, and in time the Chinese came to realize the universal validity of its teachings and to reach a correct understanding of them. But it required many centuries for such an understanding to evolve.

The men who first took the lead in introducing Buddhist concepts to China, aware of the difficulties in understanding that were involved, attempted to bridge the gap in communication by adopting the method described above, explaining the foreign doctrines in terms of words and concepts already familiar to educated Chinese from the literature of their own tradition. But they themselves were probably aware that such a method could be nothing more than a temporary makeshift. Though there were certain resemblances between the concepts of Buddhism and those of traditional Chinese philosophy, particularly of Taoism, the attempt to explain the former in terms of the latter as often as not led to distortion and misunderstanding. As the Chinese gained a deeper comprehension of the true nature of the Buddhist teachings, they came to realize that such a method of explanation was no longer appropriate and instead set about learning how to understand Buddhism on its own terms.

Thus, even before Kumarajiva's appearance in Ch'ang-an, outstanding Chinese Buddhist leaders such as Tao-an had come to realize the limitations inherent in the *ko-i* method. When the *ko-i* method was in use, for example, it had been customary to explain the Buddhist concept of *shunyata,* emptiness, which underlies the teachings of the Prajna sutras, by treating it as analogous to the Taoist concept of *wu,* or nonbeing. But as the Chinese gained a deeper understanding of Buddhist thought, they became aware that such a method of analogous explanation could never lead to a true grasp of the concept of *shunyata*. And as such important Mahayana works as the *Lotus Sutra* and the *Vimalakirti Sutra* came to be widely read, it became more evident than ever that attempts to explain their doctrines in terms of the traditional vocabulary of Confucian or Taoist thought were futile.

The fact that the Chinese Buddhists had come to realize the inadequacy of their earlier methods was no doubt one reason why they looked with such eagerness to Kumarajiva when reports of his fame reached them from the region of Central Asia.

And Kumarajiva, as we have also seen, brilliantly fulfilled their hopes and expectations. His arrival in Ch'ang-an marks the beginning of the second period of Chinese Buddhism, that designated by Kogaku Fuse as the period of schools of Buddhism. With this the *ko-i* method, which had tended to oversimplify or trivialize the loftier and more profound teachings of Buddhism, was once and for all abandoned, and for the first time the fundamental doctrines of the religion began to be expounded to the Chinese in their correct form.

The importance of Kumarajiva's contribution in making clear the differences between Hinayana and Mahayana Buddhism cannot be too strongly emphasized. During the period previous to his labors, Chinese Buddhism was, in the five levels of comparison set forth by Nichiren Daishonin, at the first or lowest level, that in which Buddhist teachings in general are weighed against those of non-Buddhist doctrines such as Confucianism and Taoism. With Kumarajiva's coming, however, the doctrines were for the first time systematically explained and the differences between the Hinayana and Mahayana elucidated. At this point, Chinese Buddhism entered the second of the five levels of comparison, that in which Hinayana and Mahayana Buddhism are weighed against each other. To be sure, many of the Mahayana sutras had already been translated into Chinese as early as the Han dynasty by scholar-monks such as Lokaraksha. But, although most of the major Mahayana texts had already been introduced to China before the time of Kumarajiva, no clear distinction was as yet made between Mahayana and Hinayana doctrines, and the true nature of the Buddhist teachings was not fully comprehended.

Two reasons may be cited to explain this state of affairs. The first is the fact that the various texts of the Buddhist canon were not necessarily introduced to China in the order in which they had come into existence in India. The early teachings of the Buddhist community in India were compiled in the form of sutras. In time, treatises and works of interpretation known as the Abhidharma texts grew up around the sutras in the various schools of early Buddhism, thus constituting the literature of Hinayana Buddhism. Later the Mahayana movement arose in reaction to what it viewed as the narrowness of the Hinayana interpretations, and with it appeared the various Mahayana sutras and the treatises that expounded and clarified their doctrines. When the first missionaries from India and Central Asia began introducing the Buddhist writings to China, however, they paid little or no attention to which writings were earlier and which later, which represented a shallower level of thought and which a more profound one, which belonged to the Hinayana division of the teachings and which to the Mahayana. Instead they introduced texts in a more or less helter-skelter fashion, concentrating upon those which were of particular interest or importance in their own eyes. Thus at times the texts were actually introduced to China in a reverse order of that in which they had appeared in India. This no doubt was one of the factors contributing to the confusion that prevailed in Buddhist circles in China.

Another was the fact that all the Buddhist sutras, whether they belonged to the Hinayana or the Mahayana division of the doctrine, invariably begin with the words "Thus have I heard," reportedly spoken by Shakyamuni's chief disciple Ananda when he related the teachings of the Buddha as he himself had heard them. That is to say, all the sutras, regardless of their date or origin, are presented as though they represented the golden words of the Buddha himself. The Chinese, having no knowledge of the long and complicated process by which the Buddhist teachings evolved and took shape in India, accepted all the writings that were brought to them as the teachings of the Buddha and had no inkling of the fact that different periods of development or different levels of profundity were represented in the different texts. The simple-hearted and unquestioning faith with which they embraced whatever writings were brought to them can only be called touching.

But there are profound differences between the Hinayana and the Mahayana teachings, and the Chinese were soon faced with the dilemma of how to explain and resolve these differences. Without being fully aware of the existence of the two great divisions of the Buddhist teachings, they could hardly conceive of how a single Buddha could have taught such varied and even contradictory doctrines, unless one supposed that he spoke in a very different manner on different occasions. To add to the perplexity, there was the confusion caused by erroneous or imperfect translations of the texts and by the fact that some of the texts purporting to have been introduced from India were in fact spurious works concocted in China.

Such, then, were the confusions and misunderstandings that prevailed in the world of Chinese Buddhism when Kumarajiva appeared in Ch'ang-an. Only by understanding the degree of darkness that characterized the age can we fully appreciate how important was Kumarajiva's contribution in dispelling confusion and bringing light to the scene.

THE ACTIVITIES OF KUMARAJIVA'S DISCIPLES

The problem of how to reconcile the differences and contradictions of the various sutras was in time resolved in a manner already suggested above, namely, by assuming that the Buddha spoke differently at different stages in his preaching, and that some of his pronouncements or systems of thought are more profound than others. But the Buddhist scholars of the time did not agree as to which sutra or sutras embodied which period of the Buddha's teachings or how the various sutras were to be ranked in terms of relative merit. These differences of opinion encouraged the formation of various schools of Buddhism, and it is this phenomenon that has led historians to designate the second phase of Chinese Buddhism as the period of the schools of Buddhism. The period lasts from Kumarajiva's entry into Ch'ang-an in 402 until 573, the year before the great persecution of Buddhism carried out by Emperor Wu of the Northern Chou dynasty (557–89). In Chinese history, it corresponds roughly to the period of the Northern and Southern Dynasties (420–589), when the Yangtze valley and the area to the south was ruled by a succession of weak Chinese dynasties with their capital at the site of present-day Nanking, and northern China was divided into states under the rule of non-Chinese peoples.

This north-south division of the country is reflected in the Buddhism of the period, and it has been customary to speak of the three schools of southern Buddhism and the seven schools of northern Buddhism. At this time, in other words, there were ten divisions in Chinese Buddhism, each putting forward its own view of the doctrine. We should not, however, think of these divisions as firmly established sects with their own distinctive creeds and practices such as were to come into existence in later centuries of Chinese Buddhism. Rather, they were individuals or small groups of individuals who, having groped about in the vast literature of Buddhism in an attempt to discover the most apt expression of the Buddha's fundamental teachings, had fixed upon one particular text or system of beliefs as worthy of the highest reverence.

The period of the schools was a time of growth and intense intellectual searching, when earnest monks of great stature and ability traveled about China studying under various teachers and carrying out religious training in different regions of the country. The seeds of this movement to bring some kind of order and systematization to the literature and teachings of Buddhism were sown by Kumarajiva in the opening years of the period of the schools of Buddhism, but his disciples brought the movement to fruition. In our discussion of Kumarajiva's translation of the *Lotus Sutra* in the preceding chapter, we have already mentioned Seng-jui, one of Kumarajiva's four major disciples, who participated in the group that produced the translation and wrote the introduction to it entitled *A Later Introduction to the Lotus Sutra*. At the beginning of that work he states: "The *Lotus Sutra* is the secret storehouse of all the Buddhas and the truest embodiment among all the sutras." He goes on to proclaim that the *Lotus Sutra* holds the highest place among all the sutras as a repository of the fundamental teachings. This was an epochal pronouncement in view of the time when it was made.

We must keep in mind that up until a short while before this the Chinese had not even been clearly aware of the distinction between the Hinayana and the Mahayana teachings. Moreover, up until the time of Kumarajiva's arrival in Ch'ang-an, the Chinese had tended to pay the highest honor to the Prajna sutras. For Seng-jui to declare that the *Lotus Sutra* was superior to the Prajna sutras and in fact represented the repository of all the essential teachings of the Buddhas was a bold move indeed. For those of us who are followers of the teachings of Nichiren Daishonin, such a view of the nature and importance of the *Lotus Sutra* seems a matter of simple truth. But, like Columbus's pronouncement that the world is round, it must have struck the people of Seng-jui's time as startling, to say the least.

Another important figure who contributed to the systematization of the Buddhist writings was Chu Tao-sheng (c. 360–434), whose experiences indicate how risky it could be at this time to take a bold stand in doctrinal matters. Nichiren Daishonin mentions him in his writings, noting that Tao-sheng was "exiled to the Su mountains," and he is also well known as one of the four major disciples of Kumarajiva. Tao-sheng, on the basis of his study of the Fa-hsien translation of the *Nirvana Sutra,* declared that all people possess the Buddha nature and that even persons of incorrigible disbelief (*icchantika*) can attain Buddhahood. The other monks of the community to which he belonged were scandalized by this pronouncement, declaring that it was not supported by the text of the *Nirvana Sutra,* and Tao-sheng was accordingly expelled from the community. He retired to a mountain in Su-chou. It is this event that Nichiren Daishonin referred to when he spoke of Tao-sheng's having been "exiled to the Su mountains." Later, when the Dharmakshema translation of the *Nirvana Sutra* was brought to southern China, it was found that Tao-sheng's view was in fact correct. The Dharmakshema translation of the sutra contained a passage, lacking in the Fa-hsien version of the text, that supported Tao-sheng's conviction.

Of more interest to us here, however, is Tao-sheng's theory of the four types of teachings put forward by the Buddha. As a means of explaining why the various sutras of the Buddhist canon seem to contradict one another, Tao-sheng put forth the view that the Buddha in the course of his preaching had expounded four different types of teachings. He did this because his listeners on different occasions had different capacities and he adjusted his preaching to the capacity of his audience. Tao-sheng held that these four types of preaching, moreover, represent an increasingly profound revelation of the truth.

Without going into detail as to the doctrinal content of each of these four types of preaching, we may note that the first and lowest level is represented by the Agama sutras of the Hinayana doctrine, which teach one to live a life of purity. Second is the level of the Prajna sutras, which reveal how one may attain nirvana through the perfection of wisdom. Third is the *Lotus Sutra,* which expounds the doctrine of the One Vehicle that makes it possible for all persons to attain Buddhahood. Fourth is the *Nirvana Sutra,* which emphasizes the eternal, personal, and pure nature of nirvana.

Though this doctrine apparently did not have any great influence upon the later development of Buddhism, it is interesting as an indication of how great was the respect shown to the *Nirvana Sutra* in southern China at this time, particularly the translation of the sutra made by Dharmakshema, mentioned above. The great popularity of this sutra proved to be only a temporary phenomenon, but it is one that must be kept in mind when considering the Buddhism of this period. As is apparent from the development of Taoist philosophy and religion in China, the Chinese have from very early times shown an intense interest in the possibility of prolonging the span of human life or even of attaining immortality. This interest has been especially strong among the ruling class, whose members have often gone to great lengths to search for elixirs of long life or other means by which to attain longevity. When the Buddhist writings, which reflect the Indian doctrine of reincarnation, were introduced to China, the Chinese supposed that reincarnation represented some kind of promise of personal immortality. They were particularly attracted to the *Nirvana Sutra,* which describes the Buddha nature inherent in all persons as eternally abiding.

To understand the Buddhist writings in this manner is of course to mistake their true import entirely. Yet one cannot help feeling that the fact that the *Nirvana Sutra* was so widely read and honored in southern China at this time is linked to this erroneous belief that it was holding forth the promise of personal immortality. So great was the popularity of the sutra that a Nirvana School based upon its doctrines flourished until the appearance of the T'ien-t'ai Sect in the sixth century.

Another important disciple of Kumarajiva who was active in southern China at this time was Hui-kuan, who died sometime around the middle of the fifth century. He too devised a theory dividing the Buddhist teachings into various categories and levels. He first divided all the sutras into two categories, those that teach the doctrine of sudden enlightenment and those that teach the doctrine of gradual enlightenment. The first category is represented by the *Flower Garland Sutra.* This he designated as the sutra of sudden enlightenment because it reveals the highest truth immediately and without recourse to any preliminary teachings. All the other sutras fall into the category of gradual enlightenment because in them the Buddha gradually and step by step moves from lower levels of truth to the highest level.

Hui-kuan divides the years of the Buddha's preaching of the teaching of gradual enlightenment into five periods spanning the time from the first sermon at Deer Park in Benares until the Buddha's death at Kushinagara. The first and most elementary level is represented by the Hinayana teachings, which hold that all phenomena have a real existence. The second, which teaches that all phenomena are empty of characteristics, is represented by the Prajna sutras. The third level is represented by the *Vimalakirti Sutra,* the fourth by the *Lotus Sutra,* and the fifth by the *Nirvana Sutra.* Like Tao-sheng, Hui-kuan views the *Nirvana Sutra* as the crowning expression of the Buddha's teachings, a further indication of the great importance that was attached to this sutra in southern China at the time.

Hui-kuan's system of classification won wide acceptance among the Buddhist scholars of the time, probably because they were already disposed to pay particular reverence to the *Nirvana Sutra.* It was advocated by such eminent monks as Seng-jou (431–94), Hui-tz'u (434–90), Chih-tsang (458–522), and Fa-yün (467–529). Chih-tsang and Fa-yün were among the most distinguished Buddhist leaders of the Liang dynasty (502–57). We may also note that Fa-yün's teacher Pao-liang (444–509) elaborated on the theory by comparing the gradual deepening of the Buddha's teachings in the five periods to the process by which milk changes its flavor as it is made into ghee, or clarified butter. He likened the five periods to the flavors of fresh milk, cream, curdled milk, butter, and ghee, a simile that was often employed in later ages.

Nearly all the followers of the Nirvana School, the San-lun, (based on a treatise by Asanga, the *Mahayana Samgraha*) or Three Treatise School, and the She-lun School—the three schools of southern Buddhism at this time—appear to have subscribed to Hui-kuan's five-period classification or some revised version of it. It was against men such as Fa-yün and the others that the Great Teacher T'ien-t'ai spoke out with such vigor, insisting that the

Lotus Sutra, not the *Nirvana Sutra,* deserved to be honored as the highest expression of the Buddhist truth.

Turning now to the situation in northern China at this time, we find that the scene was dominated by the Ti-lun School, which bases itself on Vasubandhu's commentary on one of the chapters of the *Flower Garland Sutra.* As a result, this school as well as the others of the so-called seven schools of northern China all tended to look on the *Flower Garland Sutra* as the loftiest expression of the Buddha's teachings. Hui-kuang, for example, who is regarded as the founder of the Ti-lun School, advocated a four-category division of the teachings, the first category represented by the P'i-t'an or Abhidharma School (the Hinayana teachings); the second by the Ch'eng-shih School which was based on a treatise called *The Establishment of Truth;* the third by the Prajna sutras; and the fourth by the *Nirvana Sutra* and the *Flower Garland Sutra.* This fourfold system of categorization perhaps exercised the greatest influence in northern China at the time.

In addition, Tzu-kuei, another leader of the Ti-lun School, proposed a five-part division, placing the *Nirvana Sutra* and the *Flower Garland Sutra* in separate categories, the latter in the highest position. Still another Ti-lun scholar, An-lin (507–83), set forth a six-part division, placing the *Flower Garland Sutra* in the highest place but adding to it the *Sutra of the Great Assembly,* arguing that these two works represent the most perfect expressions of the truth.

Nichiren Daishonin, writing of this period in *The Selection of the Time,* describes it as follows:

"Buddhism thus became split into ten different schools, the three schools of southern China and the seven schools of northern China. In the south there were the schools that divide the Buddha's teachings into three periods, into four periods, and into five periods, while in the north there were the northern versions of the five-period school, the school that recognized incomplete-word and complete-word teachings, the four-doctrine school, five-doctrine school, six-doctrine school, the two-Mahayana school, and the 'one-voice' school.

"Each of these schools clung fiercely to its own doctrines and clashed with the others like fire encountering water. Yet in general they shared a common view. Namely, among the various sutras preached during the Buddha's lifetime, they put the *Flower Garland Sutra* in first place, the *Nirvana Sutra* in second place, and the *Lotus Sutra* in third place. They admitted that, in comparison to such sutras as the Agamas, the Prajna sutras, the *Vimalakirti Sutra,* and the *Ssu-i Ching,* the *Lotus Sutra* represents the truth and is a complete-teachings sutra that sets forth correct views. But they held that in comparison to the *Nirvana Sutra* it represents a doctrine of non-eternity, and is an incomplete-teaching sutra that puts forth heretical views."

This, then, was the situation when the Great Teacher T'ien-t'ai appeared on the scene and, after making a study of these various theories, put forward a five-period division of his own that challenged all the others by assigning the *Lotus Sutra* to the supreme position.

5. Travelers in Search
of the Law

PILGRIMAGES OF CHINESE MONKS TO INDIA

Up to this point, we have concentrated mainly upon the process by which the Buddhist teachings were transmitted from India to the countries of Central Asia and from there to China. Here we will turn our attention to a somewhat different aspect of the history of Buddhism in East Asia, in some sense the reverse of the process referred to above, in which Chinese monks fired with a desire to gain a greater knowledge of the Buddhist doctrines made their way across Central Asia and into India.

As we have seen in earlier chapters, the Chinese were at first merely passive recipients of the Buddhist faith, at times accepting the doctrines that were brought to them by the missionaries from India and Central Asia, at times spurning them because of their foreignness. But as Buddhism spread more widely among the populace, some among its followers in China were inspired to take a more active role in the transmission of the faith, setting off on journeys to India so that they might learn more about the Buddhist teachings in the land of their origin.

Thus, for example, in 399, some two or three years before Kumarajiva's arrival in Ch'ang-an, Fa-hsien (340?–420?), the first of the famous Chinese pilgrim monks, embarked on a journey to India. Around the same time, a party headed by the monk Pao-yün set out from Central Asia. At Chang-yeh in present-day Kansu Province, the two groups joined and proceeded to India together. In 404, a few years after Fa-hsien's departure, yet another monk, Chih-meng, set out from Ch'ang-an with a group of fifteen fellow monks heading for Central Asia. Though there had earlier been Chinese who had set out for India, Fa-hsien and these other monks were the first to complete the journey successfully and to return to China with the report of their findings. Their activities, therefore, mark the beginning of a new era in the history of Chinese Buddhism.

Given the precarious travel conditions that prevailed at the time, there was no guarantee that pilgrims who set out beyond the far western borders of China would ever return to their native land alive. The monks who embarked on the long journey to India were, in the words on the *Lotus Sutra,* "risking life and limb." It was probably in some degree the very danger and challenge of the trip that inspired so many men of the time to undertake it.

To better understand why these members of the Buddhist community in China should have been impelled to essay the perilous trip to India, let us examine some of the motives that underlay their action. By the end of the fourth century Buddhism had won a firm place in the spiritual life of the Chinese people, and the journeys of the Chinese monk-pilgrims are an outcome and expression of the ardor that marked the Chinese Buddhist community at this time. Moreover, as we have seen in the case of Kumarajiva, the Chinese Buddhists were eager to make contact with outstanding teachers of India and Central Asia so that they might gain a more accurate understanding of the doctrines of their faith, and this was no doubt one of the objectives that inspired the journeys. Finally, during the third and fourth centuries the number of religious establishments and of monks and nuns in China had grown very rapidly. With this rapid growth had come a certain relaxation in the rules governing the religious community, and signs of moral laxity and decay had begun to appear. One of the reasons for making the pilgrimage to India was to obtain a more thorough and accurate knowledge of the vinaya, or rules of religious discipline, so that order could be restored to the Chinese Buddhist community.

This last in particular was a motive in the case of Fa-hsien, as is made clear in his biography, *The Account of Fa-hsien,* a work based on Fa-hsien's own writings and known also as *The Record of Buddhist Countries.* There it is stated: "When Fa-hsien was still in Ch'ang-an, he was much distressed at the gaps and deficiencies in the texts dealing with the rules of religious discipline. For that reason, in the first year of the Hung-shih era, the year with the cyclical sign *chi-hai* [A.D. 399], he finally set out in company with Hui-ching, Tao-cheng, Hui-ying, Hui-wei, and others, all of them pledged to a common purpose, determined to journey to India and seek the rules of discipline."

Mahayana Buddhism was in its origin largely a movement centered about men and women believers of the lay community and from the beginning had a tendency to pay less attention to the rules of monastic discipline than did Theravada or Hinayana Buddhism. Moreover, the monastic groups that took shape in China were quite different in their organization from the Sangha, or Buddhist monastic order, as it had existed in India. One may wonder, therefore, why Fa-hsien should have been so deeply concerned about journeying to India and obtaining copies of the rules of monastic discipline. Any community of monks or nuns, however, or for that matter, any organization of lay believers, must have rules and regulations to govern their members' activities as Buddhist believers and as human beings. This holds true for any time or place. Fa-hsien no doubt felt that the rules in force in Chinese communities were inadequate and had determined to do what he could to remedy the situation.

Kumarajiva shared this concern and, soon after he entered Ch'ang-an early in 402, set about energetically translating the rules of discipline and in 403 began to translate the *Rules of Discipline in Ten Categories,* the vinaya of the Sarvastivada School, in sixty-one volumes. This indicates how strong was the desire on the part of the Buddhist community in China to gain a complete and accurate knowledge of the rules of monastic life.

The Chinese government authorities on a number of occasions took steps to restrict Buddhist activities or to suppress the religion entirely, and their excuse for doing so was always the degeneracy and disorder that prevailed among the members of the monastic community. Thus, for example, they would charge that the temples were concealing hoards of weapons, engaging in illegal manufacture of wine, or violating the vows of celibacy. Charges of this kind, of course, were not the real reasons for such movements to persecute the Buddhist faith. These were to be found much deeper, in the age-old hostility that Confucian and Taoist institutions and ways of thought manifested toward the foreign religion. As Buddhism continued to spread rapidly throughout Chinese society, these groups, particularly the members of the Taoist clergy, lost no opportunity to plot against the Buddhists and to incite the government authorities into taking steps to harass them. If there had been no corruption or moral laxity within Buddhist monastic circles, the groups hostile to Buddhism would probably have discovered some other excuse to launch their attacks. But evidences of moral corruption in the monastic community provided them with an ideal opportunity for attack, because rumors of scandalous activities could be used with great effectiveness to arouse the general populace, whose alms supported the monastic establishments, and turn them against the Buddhist organizations.

Before leaving this discussion of monastic discipline, I would like to stress one important fact, namely, that strict adherence to the rules of religious discipline alone does not constitute the whole of Buddhist practice. In other words, abiding by the rules of discipline is not an end in itself, but merely one step in the process toward realization of the Way of Buddhism. The Chinese, with their long history and high level of cultural development, no doubt realized this, which is one reason why Hinayana Buddhism, with its primary emphasis upon monastic rules of conduct, never made any significant progress in China.

FA-HSIEN'S ACCOUNT OF HIS TRAVELS AND ITS IMPORTANCE

Fa-hsien, as we have seen, set out on a pilgrimage to the birthplace of Buddhism in India in order to gain a more thorough knowledge of the texts on religious discipline. The journey took him some fourteen years to complete, and he accomplished the purpose for which he had set out, returning to China in 414 with a copy of the rules of discipline of the Mahasamghika School. Working with another monk, he produced a Chinese translation of the text in forty volumes entitled *Mo-ho-seng-chih Lü.*

But, important as this labor may have been to the people of his own time, Fa-hsien has been remembered by later ages for somewhat different reasons. His contribution to the history of Buddhism lies first of all in the fact that, having embarked upon such a lengthy and ambitious journey, he was able to carry it through to completion. It is estimated that he was around sixty years old when he set out in 399, scarcely an age at which most people would care to face the trials of a long and arduous trip. Leaving China, he proceeded westward across the Taklamakan Desert, crossed the steep slopes of the Pamirs, and then, after negotiating the so-called Hanging Passage—a series of scaffoldings and suspension bridges through the otherwise impassable gorges of the upper Indus River—he at last made his way into India. It took him a total of six years merely to get from China to India.

After spending another six years in India, he embarked on the journey home, choosing to go by the sea route. Boarding a merchant vessel at the mouth of the Ganges, he proceeded to the island kingdom of Simhala (Sri Lanka), where he remained for two years acquiring copies of Buddhist scriptures. From there he proceeded east by ship, but was forced by storms to stop at an island, probably Sumatra or Java. There he transferred to another ship and sailed north to the China coast, landing at Ch'ing-chou in Shantung. He was most likely around seventy-seven when he at last returned to his native land.

When we think of Chinese monks who journeyed to India, we

tend to think first of all of Hsüan-tsang (602–64), perhaps because he figures so prominently in the famous Chinese historical romance *Journey to the West*. But we should not forget that over two hundred years before Hsüan-tsang made his trip to India, Fa-hsien had already accomplished the feat.

Both Fa-hsien and Hsüan-tsang left invaluable accounts of their travels, and their names and exploits are well known to posterity. But I like to reflect on all the other Chinese monks who likewise set out for India in search of the essence of the Buddhist Law, who died along the way or whose names and deeds for one reason or another have not been handed down to us. They, if in spirit only, helped to contribute to the advancement of Buddhism as much as did the more renowned figures such as Fa-hsien and Hsüan-tsang. All these men, the known and the unknown alike, were fired with the same religious ardor and determination, and it was due to their unflagging efforts that Buddhism was able to make the passage from India to China and thence to Korea and Japan, and to become the major world religion that it is today. We can only stand in awe before their courage and devotion to the faith.

Fa-hsien visited a total of twenty-seven states in the course of his travels. In the account that he kept of his journey, he has left a terse but highly informative record of the states that existed in Central Asia and India in the early years of the fifth century. His work is therefore of inestimable value to scholars engaged in the study of the history and geography of the area and has been translated numerous times into Western languages. Fa-hsien's primary concern, of course, was to reach India and gain a greater knowledge of the Buddhist teachings and texts. He probably never dreamed that the brief notes which he kept of his journey would be so highly prized by scholars of later times. In spite of the immense distance that he covered in his journey, his account runs to less than ten thousand characters in the Chinese original. But it is perhaps the very economy and succinctness of his observations that gives such force to his narrative.

Needless to say, Fa-hsien's account of his journey became required reading for all those in later ages who aspired to make a similar pilgrimage in search of the Law. Indeed, the book may well have inspired monks who had not previously considered making such a journey. For all later monks setting out for India such as Hsüan-tsang and I-ching (635–713), Fa-hsien's text served as a guidebook along the way. Thus I-ching, in the opening words of his own travel account, *The Account of the Eminent T'ang Monks Who Journeyed to the Western Region in Search of the Law,* acknowledges his debt to Fa-hsien by saying, "It was Master Fa-hsien who first opened up the road through the wilderness."

Another thing that makes Fa-hsien's *Record of Buddhist Countries* of such great significance is the fact that it preserves an account of the lands of India and Central Asia at a time when Buddhism was at the height of its influence and prosperity in those regions. The propagation of the Buddhist teachings, the *kosen-rufu* movement, if you will, that had begun in India in Shakyamuni's time, had reached its peak of development in these areas in the fourth and early fifth centuries. By contrast, the account left us by Hsüan-tsang, who visited the same area in the seventh century, shows us Buddhism in a period of decline and is tinged with a note of autumnal sadness.

Fa-hsien, writing of the flourishing condition of Buddhism, states: "From the river of flowing sands on west, in all the lands of India the rulers are fervent believers in the Buddhist faith. When the ruler offers alms to the monastic community, he removes his royal crown and, in company with the members of his family and his officials and statesmen, offers the food with his own hands. After the meal is concluded, he spreads a carpet on the ground and takes his seat there before the monks, who sit in the place of honor. The ruler does not venture to sit in a chair himself. This ceremony by which the ruler offers alms has probably been handed down from the time of the Buddha to the present day."

The "river of flowing sands" refers to the desert region at the far western end of the Gobi Desert, and we can therefore see from Fa-hsien's account that the entire region of Central Asia and the Indian subcontinent was at this time under the sway of the Buddhist religion. There is no reason to doubt that the rulers and citizens of the states in this region were ardent supporters of the Buddhist Law and paid honor to the members of the monastic community in much the manner Fa-hsien indicates.

One very important aspect of Fa-hsien's account is that in the course of his travels through over twenty different states he did not once encounter an incident of warfare or military strife. These states of Central Asia and India, one of the great cultural cross-roads of the world, were all firm adherents of the Buddhist faith and appear to have carried on their cultural relations in perfect peace. This is a fact of history that has too often been forgotten in later ages. Fa-hsien seems not only to have been able to travel freely and without danger, but actually to have received material assistance from the rulers of the states through which he passed. Supplied in this way with the food and traveling equipment that he needed, he was able to move across the desert regions from one oasis state to another until he reached his destination in India. In Fa-hsien's time there were no facilities for public transportation, and the geography of the regions that he traveled presented difficulties and perils at every turn. But because the states through which he passed were all supporters of the Buddhist faith and because peace prevailed in the area, he was able to pursue his arduous journey to a successful conclusion. Fa-hsien and the others of his party carried no passports, as travelers do nowadays. Their status as Buddhist monks was all the passport they needed to insure that they would be welcomed and assisted on their way at every stage of the journey.

We may note with regret that today, if one were to attempt to follow the same route that Fa-hsien took, he would find his way repeatedly impeded by the barriers of modern nationalism and bureaucratic red tape.

Over Endless Mountains and Rivers

Let us turn now to Fa-hsien's own account and see just what was involved in a pilgrimage to India at the beginning of the fifth century.

Fa-hsien and his party, setting out in the spring of 399 from Ch'ang-an, the capital of the Later Ch'in dynasty, proceeded westward over the Lung Mountains to the little state of Ch'ien-kuei, where they spent the period of summer religious retreat. From there they traveled to a state called Nu-t'an, crossed the Yang-lou Mountains, and reached the Chinese outpost at Chang-yeh. Here they joined up with the monks Chih-yen, Hui-chien, Seng-shao, Pao-yün, and Seng-ching, who had been traveling separately. They were later joined at Yü-t'ien, or Khotan, by Hui-ta, bringing the party to a total of eleven members. Later, some of these eleven abandoned the journey and turned back to China, some for one reason or another remained behind in the states through which the group passed while still others died along the way.

Wherever there were human settlements, the travelers seem to have been welcomed with a warmth and goodwill that one could scarcely hope to enjoy in our modern society. On the other hand, once they emerged from these settlements to face the hardships of the open road, they encountered almost indescribable dangers and trials. Having made their way to Tun-huang, the far western outpost famous for its Buddhist caves and sculpture, they were supplied with provisions by Li Sung, the prefect of the region, and from there set out across the desert.

Fa-hsien, in a passage already cited earlier, describes the scene is this way: "The sands are full of evil spirits and burning winds, and anyone who encounters them dies; no one is left unharmed. No birds fly overhead, no animals run across the ground. Squint one's eyes, gaze as one may in the four directions, he can find no place to turn, nothing to guide him; only the dried bones of the dead serve as markers of the trail." This often-quoted passage gives us some idea of the frightful conditions faced by the travelers. Only men fortified by ardent courage and faith and a burning determination to reach their objective could bring themselves to press ahead under such circumstances. We can only bow our heads in respect before these pilgrim monks who, never succumbing to the temptation to turn back, pushed forward on their journey to India, as well as before the monks of India and the countries of Central Asia who, crossing the same treacherous desert wastes in an eastward direction, journeyed to China in order to spread a knowledge of the Buddhist teachings there.

Fa-hsien and his party, after traveling for seventeen days over the desert sands, reached the oasis state of Shan-shan near the lake Lop Nor and the site of the earlier state of Lou-lan. According to Fa-hsien, the ruler of Shan-shan was a strong supporter of Buddhism. There were over four thousand Buddhist monks in the state, all of them devoted to the study of the Hinayana teachings. From there the party proceeded northwest to the state of Wu-i, or Karashahr, which also had a thriving Buddhist community of over four thousand monks who adhered to the Hinayana teachings and observed the rules of monastic discipline with great strictness.

The next major stop for the party was the state of Khotan on the southern route through the region. Khotan, along with Kumarajiva's native state of Kucha on the northern route, was one of the most flourishing countries in Central Asia at this time. "The land is very prosperous and happy," writes Fa-hsien, "and its people are numerous and thriving. All of them are followers of the Buddhist Law and delight in practicing its teachings. The monks number several tens of thousands, the majority of them dedicated to Mahayana doctrines. They all receive food and alms from the ruler of the kingdom. The people of the state live scattered here and there like so many stars, and each household has a small stupa or pagoda erected in front of its gate."

Fa-hsien and his party remained in Khotan for a period of three months. Partly they did so in order to be able to witness an important festival in which Buddhist images were paraded through the streets. But I like to imagine that Fa-hsien felt himself almost irresistibly drawn to the peaceful and pious atmosphere of Khotan. After leaving China, which at this time was torn by strife and warfare, and traveling over the forbidding desert regions, it must have seemed to him as though, arriving at this green oasis, he had miraculously chanced upon a utopian society where Buddhism flourished, the country was peaceful and prosperous, and the people rejoiced in the Law. If Fa-hsien and the others of his party had not been committed to their goal of reaching India, they might well have felt that there was no reason to press farther on their perilous journey and have been tempted to remain indefinitely in this admirable land.

Spurred on by their hopes of reaching India, however, Fa-hsien and his party continued westward. After tramping for twenty-five days through the Taklamakan Desert, they arrived at the oasis of Tzu-ho, or Karghalik. The ruler of this state, too, was a devotee of the Buddhist Way, and his country contained over a thousand monks who were adherents of Mahayana Buddhism. Fa-hsien and his companions remained there for fifteen days while they made preparations for crossing the Ts'ung-ling, or Pamir, Mountains.

The Pamirs constitute a high plateau where the Hindu Kush, Tien Shan, and Himalayan mountain ranges converge. The plateau averages four thousand meters in height, well over the height of Mount Fuji. It serves as the east-west watershed for eastern Asia and poses incalculable hardships for travelers, great numbers of whom have lost their lives there.

Fa-hsien writes: "The Ts'ung-ling ranges are covered with snow both winter and summer. They are inhabited by poison dragons. If one arouses the ill humor of the dragons, they will at once call forth poisonous winds, cause the snow to fall, or send showers of sand, gravel, and stones flying. Of the persons who have encountered such difficulties, hardly one in ten thousand has escaped uninjured. The inhabitants of the region refer to the poison dragons as the Snow Mountain people."

It is estimated that Fa-hsien was around sixty-five years of age when he crossed these formidable mountains. He was carried forward by his fervent desire to set eyes upon India before he died. No doubt the intense religious faith that impelled him forward had allowed him to reach a state of mind that transcended the concepts of life and death. At the same time, having come this far, he no doubt realized that there was no possibility of turning back and that the only course open to him was to advance step by step toward the homeland of the Buddha. Fully prepared to sacrifice life and limb, he pushed onward over the steep peaks.

Along the way he and his party stopped in the state of Yü-mo, or Mamuk, to spend the period of summer religious retreat. From there they proceeded to the state of Chieh-ch'a, or Tashkurghan, where they observed the ceremony at which the ruler presented alms to the Buddhist monks of his realm. Proceeding onward, they reached T'o-li, or Darel, a state devoted to Hinayana Buddhism. They were now in the region of northern India.

But before them still loomed one of the most difficult stretches of the entire journey, the so-called Hanging Passage through the gorges of the upper Indus River. Of this Fa-hsien writes: "The trail is precarious and the cliffs and escarpments are sheer, the mountains forming stone walls that plunge thousands of meters to the valley below. Peering down, one's eyes grow dizzy, and when one tries to push forward, he can find no spot to place his foot." The party had to make their way along the face of the sheer cliff by means of a series of scaffoldings and suspension bridges, negotiating some seven hundred difficult spots in the process.

Fa-hsien notes that even such famous earlier Chinese travelers to Central Asia as Chang Ch'ien in the second century B.C. or Kan Ying in the first century A.D. had not succeeded in journeying this far. Fa-hsien was surely justified in speaking with pride of his exploits, for he was the first in the long centuries of Chinese history to accomplish such a lengthy and challenging expedition.

Having traversed the Hanging Passage, the pilgrims now found the plain of Gandhara, the most flourishing center of Buddhist activities in all of India at that time, stretching before their eyes. Their long months and years of painful journeying had at last brought them to their destination.

They first entered the state of Wu-ch'ang, or Udyana, and then proceeded south to the state of Su-ho-to, or Swat. In time they reached the kingdom of Gandhara itself, and thereafter proceeded to visit other important Buddhist kingdoms of northwestern India such as Taxila and Peshawar. At this point three members of the party, Hui-ta, Pao-yün and Seng-ching, took leave of Fa-hsien and the others and set out on the journey back to China.

Pao-yün succeeded in returning to China, and something is known of his later activities there. In Ch'ang-an he studied under Buddhabhadra (359–429), also known as Chüeh-hsien, a priest from northern India who came to China in 406. Later, when Buddhabhadra moved to a temple in Chien-k'ang (present-day Nanking), Pao-yün accompanied him there. Some years later, when Fa-hsien returned alone by sea from his prolonged journey, he stopped at this temple and there the former fellow travelers Fa-hsien and Pao-yün had a dramatic reunion. After all the trials and adventures that had befallen them in the intervening years, it must have been a deeply moving occasion for the two men. One feels there must have been some deep bond of fate linking the two that brought them together again after their years of separation and distant wandering.

After parting from Pao-yün and the others at Peshawar, Fa-hsien and his party made their way to the state of Nagarahara, near modern Jalalabad. Having passed the three winter months there, they proceeded south over the Little Snow Mountains, the Sefid-Kuh range. As they made their way over the snowy slopes, they encountered fierce blasts of icy wind and the whole party were rendered speechless with terror and exhaustion. Suddenly one member of the group, Hui-ching, began frothing at the mouth and announced that he could not go any farther, begging the others to press on without him. He died shortly after. Fa-hsien, bending over him and weeping bitterly, lamented the fate that had not permitted the monk to live until he reached the homeland of the Buddha.

This kind of scene must have occurred with tragic frequency during the arduous pilgrimages made by Chinese monks to Central Asia and India. It is appropriate that we should pause a moment in silent respect to consider the sacrifices that they made in order that Buddhism might become a great world religion.

VISITING THE HOLY SITES OF BUDDHISM

Fa-hsien proceeded on his way, visiting sites in central and southern India associated with the Buddha and his disciples. His description, brief though it is, provides valuable information on the condition of Indian Buddhism at this time and helps to supplement the otherwise rather scanty sources on Indian history and society in these early times.

Moving southward, Fa-hsien entered the region of central India, which he describes as mild in climate and free of frost and snow. Visiting the state of Mathura, he remarks upon the happy and prosperous condition of the population and the fact that they were not subjected to harsh laws or penalties. They were free to move about, change their place of residence, and open up new lands for cultivation at will and were not required to register with the government officials. Most offenses were punished by the mere exaction of a fine, and even serious crimes called for no more than the amputation of the right hand. The death penalty was apparently unknown. Buddhism was highly honored in the state, and the ruler and all his ministers were followers of the faith. The monks numbered three thousand and there were twenty monasteries in the area. The people did not drink alcoholic beverages or eat meat.

In describing the monastic communities, Fa-hsien mentions that they included stupas or pagodas dedicated to the Buddha's major disciples such as Shariputra, Maudgalyayana, and Ananda or to each of the three divisions of the Buddhist canon—the sutras, the rules of discipline, and the treatises. Shariputra was known as "foremost in wisdom" among Shakyamuni's ten major disciples, while Maudgalyayana was known as "foremost in magical powers," and presumably one paid reverence to the pagodas dedicated to these disciples in hopes of excelling in the same manner that they had. In the case of the pagoda dedicated to Ananda, Fa-hsien tells us that it was reverenced by large numbers of nuns because Ananda was said to have been the one who persuaded Shakyamuni to allow women to enter the Buddhist Order.

The groups worshipping the pagodas were probably followers

of Hinayana Buddhism. In addition, Fa-hsien mentions that there were adherents of the Mahayana teachings who paid reverence to the concept of prajna (wisdom) and to the bodhisattvas Manjushri and Avalokiteshvara. The monks of Mathura, Fa-hsien notes, were permitted to take certain types of liquid food such as honey or broths made of grain or beans after the midday meal. This practice was forbidden among followers of the Hinayana teachings but permitted among the Mahayanists, and it would therefore appear that the state of Mathura in general adhered to Mahayana practices.

Fa-hsien's next stop was the state of Sankisa, where he observed a community of some one thousand monks and nuns eating together and studying both the Hinayana and Mahayana teachings. Following that, he visited Kanauj, which had two monastic establishments, both devoted entirely to Hinayana teachings.

Finally he arrived at Savatthi, the capital of the state of Koshala or Kosala. Shakyamuni had resided in Savatthi for approximately twenty-five years and had carried out some of his most vigorous missionary activity there. Savatthi was also the site of the famous Jetavana Monastery, which was built for the monks of the Buddhist Order by the wealthy merchant Sudatta so that they would have a retreat in which to spend the rainy season. The Buddha, using this as a base for his activities, engaged in debates with the exponents of other religious doctrines and preached to the ruler of the kingdom, his ministers, and the population in general.

As a result of these missionary activities, it is said that one third of the inhabitants of the city were converted to the Buddhist teachings. At the same time, however, it is clear that there were many hostile elements among the population, as we can see from the difficulties and persecutions that Shakyamuni was obliged to endure. These include slanderous rumors spread by the Brahmans of the city that Shakyamuni had fathered a child by a courtesan, or had arranged for the murder of another courtesan with whom he had been carrying on an affair. And some years later, when a ruler named Vidudabha came to the throne of Kosala, he attacked Shakyamuni's native state and wiped out all the members of the

Shakya clan. Savatthi was not only a scene of religious triumph for the Buddha but a source of suffering and sorrow as well.

In his account of Savatthi, Fa-hsien discourses at some length on the Buddha's activities. But as he looked out over the site of the city a thousand years or more after the death of Shakyamuni, he found the population reduced to some two hundred or more households and the once great city no more than a ruin. The sight filled him with thoughts of the impermanence of all things. Fa-hsien, speaking of himself in the third person, writes: "When Fa-hsien and Tao-cheng arrived at the Jetavana Monastery, they recalled that the World-honored One had lived there for twenty-five years. They themselves had been born in a faraway barbarian region and with their companions had journeyed onward from state to state. Along the way, some of the members of their group had gone back to China, while others, as they recalled with pain, had died on the road. And now, as they arrived at this spot and gazed at these remains of the place where the Buddha had once been, they were filled with sorrow and grieved in their hearts."

Pushing eastward, Fa-hsien arrived at Kapilavastu, the place where Shakyamuni Buddha was born and spent his youthful years. But this city too had fallen into sad decline in the centuries since the Buddha's passing. "Within the city there was no sign of a ruler or his subjects, everything being reduced to ruin," writes Fa-hsien. "All to be found there were some twenty or thirty dwellings belonging to monks or laymen." Once again he must have been struck with the transient nature of all phenomena.

Some miles east of the city of Kapilavastu was Lumbini, the site of the royal gardens where Shakyamuni's mother, Queen Maya, gave birth to him beside a pool. Fa-hsien visited this spot as well, observing the pool, which was used as a source of drinking water by the monks in the area. He concludes his description of Kapilavastu on a cautionary note, saying: "The state of Kapilavastu is in ruined condition. There are very few inhabitants, and white elephants and lions stalk the roads in a terrifying manner. It is no place in which to travel about idly."

Continuing eastward, he visited Kushinagara, the place where the Buddha died, made his way southeast to Vaishali, the home of the Licchavi tribe, and then, proceeding south across the Ganges, arrived at Pataliputra, the capital of the state of Magadha. This was the capital of the famous Buddhist ruler King Ashoka, and was one of the wealthiest and most flourishing cities in all of central India at the time, containing temples devoted to the Mahayana teachings.

Magadha had been a very important supporter of Buddhism even during the lifetime of the Buddha. Its ruler at that time, King Bimbisara, was an enthusiastic follower of Shakyamuni's teachings. King Bimbisara's son and successor, King Ajatashatru, also provided support and encouragement to the Buddhist Order after Shakyamuni's death. Of the so-called sixteen kingdoms mentioned in the Buddhist scriptures as existing in India in Shakyamuni's time, Magadha had the closest ties with the Buddhist religion.

King Ajatashatru, who came to the throne of Magadha some seven years before the Buddha's death, began a policy of expansion which was carried on by his successors until, under the Mauryan dynasty, all of India was united under one rule. This process of unification was brought to completion by the third and greatest of the Mauryan rulers, King Ashoka, who probably came to the throne around 268 B.C. He was a devout follower of Buddhism, and Buddhist ideals are clearly reflected in his government policies.

After describing the flourishing condition of Pataliputra and the Buddhist sites and ceremonies there, Fa-hsien records his visit to Rajagaha, the capital of Magadha in the Buddha's time, and to Mount Gridhrakuta, or Eagle Peak, the spot on the outskirts of the city where Shakyamuni is said to have preached on various occasions to his disciples and followers. Fa-hsien then made trips to the south and west so as to be able to visit Buddh Gaya, the place where Shakyamuni attained enlightenment, and Deer Park at Sarnath, near the city of Benares, where he first began his preaching of the Law. Thus Fa-hsien, in spite of his advanced age, which at this time was probably around seventy, was able to carry to completion his ambitious plan to journey to India and view the places associated with the founder of his faith.

The return journey to China by ship proved to be no less trying than the journey by land, and it was three years before Fa-hsien reached the shores of his native country.

After returning to China, Fa-hsien took up residence in Chien-k'ang, the present-day city of Nanking, and devoted himself to the task of translating the sacred texts and writings on monastic discipline that he had brought back with him. He is said to have died at a temple called Hsin-ssu in Ching-chou. Some sources give his age as eighty-two at the time of his death, others as eighty-six. Whichever is correct, there is no doubt that he was very advanced in age when his rich and eventful life came to a close.

6. Nan-yüeh Hui-ssu and the Veneration of the *Lotus Sutra*

THE BEGINNINGS OF THE T'IEN-T'AI SCHOOL

In the preceding chapters we have traced the process by which Buddhism was introduced to China by missionaries from India and Central Asia. We have examined the activities of the translators who worked to make available to Chinese readers the vast literature of Hinayana and Mahayana Buddhism. We have seen the growth of various schools of Buddhism as the Chinese Buddhists labored to absorb this huge body of doctrine and to systematize it and impose some kind of hierarchical order upon its varied teachings. And we have noted the activities of the Chinese monks who, seeking a fuller and more accurate understanding of the Buddhist Law, made the perilous journey to India in search of teachers and texts.

We now enter the third period of the five-period division of Chinese Buddhism proposed by the Japanese scholar Kogaku Fuse. Fuse designates it the eclectic or syncretic period, since during it the so-called seven schools of northern China and three schools of southern China sought to understand each other's teachings and combine them into a higher level of interpretation. Fuse sees the period as beginning around 575. One may question whether "eclectic period" is the most appropriate designation for this era or just what date should be regarded as its starting point, but these are questions we will not go into here.

In the chapters that follow, I will not attempt to deal with the entire range of Buddhist activities in China or to trace the development of all the various schools of Chinese Buddhism. Instead, I will concentrate upon the line of development that led to the establishment of the T'ien-t'ai Sect of Buddhism, which honors the *Lotus Sutra* as the highest expression of the Buddhist Law. This is the sect of Chinese Buddhism that is of greatest importance to followers of the teachings of Nichiren Daishonin, and in most of the chapters that follow, it will be the focus of my discussion.

The Great Teacher Miao-lo (711–82), a major scholar of the T'ien-t'ai Sect in T'ang times, describes the school as originating in the teachings of the great Indian Buddhist philosopher Nagarjuna. Miao-lo then goes on to name three Chinese monk-scholars who step by step developed the T'ien-t'ai teachings and brought them to completion: Hui-wen, Nan-yüeh Hui-ssu (515–77), and T'ien-t'ai Chih-i (538–97). These three are customarily regarded as the first three patriarchs of the T'ien-t'ai School in China and their teachings and activities will be the subject of my narrative in this and the following chapter.

Little is known about Hui-wen, and the dates of his birth and death cannot be determined. He was a native of northern China and flourished in the time of the Northern Ch'i dynasty, which ruled the area of northeastern China from 550 to 577. By studying the *Treatise on the Middle Way* and the *Treatise on the Larger Perfection of Wisdom* by Nagarjuna, he is said to have established a practice known as the threefold contemplation in a single mind by which enlightenment could be achieved. If Nagarjuna is regarded as the founder of the T'ien-t'ai School as a whole, then Hui-wen is counted as the second rather than the first patriarch.

Because of the paucity of sources, we can say no more than this about Hui-wen. To get some idea of the meaning and importance of his thought, we must see how it was elaborated and put into practice by his disciple and successor in the T'ien-t'ai line, Hui-ssu.

HUI-SSU AND HIS UNDERSTANDING OF THE *Lotus Sutra*

We are fortunate in having much more detailed information about Hui-ssu and his ideas. *Further Biographies of Eminent Monks* by the T'ang monk Tao-hsüan (596–667) contains an account of him, and his own writings include the autobiographical work entitled *Writing Setting Forth My Vow* as well as various doctrinal works.

Hui-ssu was born in Wu-chin in present-day Honan Province in 515, in the area of China that was at that time ruled by the Northern Wei dynasty. As a child he is said to have been noted for his kindness and gentleness and to have enjoyed great praise in the community where he lived.

He became a monk at the age of fifteen. According to his own account, he spent the next ten years diligently reading and memorizing the *Lotus Sutra* and other Mahayana sutras and practicing various kinds of religious austerities. His biography states that he ate only one meal a day, declined any kind of special alms or offerings, and refused all attempts to make special arrangements for him or treat him with marks of courtesy. In the course of several years, he is said to have read through the *Lotus Sutra* and other works (some thirty volumes or more) a total of one thousand times. From this it is apparent that in his youthful years he imposed upon himself a very rigorous course of training.

According to Hui-ssu's own account, he was moved to enter the Buddhist clergy by the sight of so many persons dying around him, which impressed upon him the transitory nature of human life. Aroused to feelings of pity and compassion, he determined to follow the path of the bodhisattva and to do what he could to relieve the sufferings of his fellow beings.

The period of disunity that prevailed in China at this time was marked by great strife and unrest, and the common people of the time were no doubt subjected to extreme hardship by the political instability that prevailed. Moreover, the Northern Wei dynasty (386–535), under which Hui-ssu lived in his childhood years, was faltering to its end, and around 534 split into two states, the Western Wei (535–57) and the Eastern Wei (534–50). Hui-ssu must have witnessed many scenes of bloodshed and misery during these troubled times. His response to the suffering around him was to set out in search of the Way so that he might dispel the ignorance of the men and women of his time and lead them to salvation. In Buddhism, one does not embark on the search for truth merely so that one may accomplish one's own emancipation and satisfy one's own longings for spiritual peace. The true practitioner of the Buddhist teachings is one who seeks to bring to all men and women the kind of truth or doctrine that enables them to carry out a basic and thoroughgoing revolution within their own lives, thus freeing them from doubt and affliction. This was the goal that Hui-ssu had in mind when he embarked on his own search for the Way.

After his ten years of extensive study, Hui-ssu began journeying in search of a teacher. As he himself relates, he traveled about the area of northern China, visiting the great Buddhist teachers of the time and studying the doctrines of Mahayana under them. He devoted particular attention to the practice of meditation, for a period of some seven years moving about and studying under one meditation master after another, hoping to experience for himself the essence of the Buddhist teachings and undergo true enlightenment. This was during the years from the age of twenty-four or twenty-five to thirty-one or thirty-two.

At this time, the Buddhism of southern China was marked by a strong emphasis upon the study of Buddhist texts and an exegetical approach to the religion. In contrast to this theoretical and scholarly approach, the Buddhism of northern China stressed the practice of meditation and sutra recitation. Hui-ssu, brought up in the ways of northern Buddhism, believed that the Buddhist teachings were not doctrines to be apprehended intellectually but truths that one could experience and affirm within one's own life, and he set about pursuing them through the practice of meditation.

In the course of his travels, Hui-ssu came to study under Hui-wen, probably when he was about the age of thirty-two. As we have seen earlier, Hui-wen followed the teachings of Nagarjuna, laying particular stress on Nagarjuna's encyclopedic work, the *Treatise on the Larger Perfection of Wisdom.* It was under Hui-wen's guidance that Hui-ssu attained true enlightenment.

During the first year of his study under Hui-wen, though Hui-ssu pursued his goal with great diligence, he was not able to gain enlightenment. It was not until the following summer, when Hui-ssu applied himself to intensive meditation, that he at last grasped the true meaning of the *Lotus Sutra.* According to his biography in the *Further Biographies of Eminent Monks,* his enlightenment came at the very end of the summer, when he was feeling deeply discouraged because he had made so little progress under Hui-wen and was shamed and grieved at the meaninglessness of his life. As he was about to lean against a wall in despair, understanding suddenly came to him in a flash and instantly he was able to comprehend the *"Lotus Sutra* meditation" he had been trying to master and the Mahayana teachings.

Some fifteen years had passed since Hui-ssu first took the tonsure and became a monk. He had read and recited the *Lotus Sutra* and the other Mahayana sutras numberless times. He had mastered the Hinayana meditation techniques and gone on to master those of the Mahayana as well, and for years had subjected himself to the most rigorous discipline. But until the moment when he at last wakened to the true significance of the *Lotus Sutra,* he had been unable to gain enlightenment and had felt to his great shame that his life was passing in a futile and profitless fashion.

From this it is apparent that no matter how many times one may read the words of the *Lotus Sutra,* if one fails to grasp the deeper significance that lies behind them, then the action is all but meaningless. It also indicates that no matter what sort of severe and taxing religious practices one engages in, no matter how many years he may devote himself to meditation, he cannot hope in that way to gain true enlightenment. Only if he places himself under the guidance of a teacher who possesses a full and correct understanding of the Buddhist doctrines can he reach the highest level of enlightenment.

True enlightenment is something that one must realize for himself in the context of his own life. But in order to reach the point at which such realization becomes possible, he must have the guidance of a genuinely reliable teacher. The ten or fifteen years during which Hui-ssu practiced austerities and wandered here and there represent a process of preparation leading up to the encounter with such a teacher.

THE *Lotus Sutra* MEDITATION

Hui-ssu, when he gained enlightenment, reached a comprehension of the "*Lotus Sutra* meditation." Here we must ask just what is meant by this phrase *Lotus Sutra* samadhi, or meditation (*Fa-hua san-mei*).

Hui-ssu wrote a work entitled *The Significance of the Peaceful Practices Chapter of the Lotus Sutra*. In this work, he describes religious practices based on the *Lotus Sutra*. He states that a person seeking to understand the *Lotus Sutra* should engage in two types of meditation, meditation or acts of devotion involving overt practices such as sutra recitation, and silent meditation that has no outward manifestation. Hui-ssu particularly recommends the latter type of meditation practice as it is set forth in the "Peaceful Practices" chapter (chapter 14) of the *Lotus Sutra*.

Hui-ssu's *Lotus Sutra* meditation is simply a type of practice that one carries out in order to gain understanding of the true significance of the *Lotus Sutra*. Specifically, it is a period of religious practice lasting for twenty-one days during which one recites the *Lotus Sutra* and carries out other actions, and at the same time devotes oneself to silent meditation.

The term *Fa-hua san-mei* appears in the *Lotus Sutra* itself, in two different chapters. In chapter 27, it is mentioned in connection with a bodhisattva named Pure Eyes who, we are told, "had for a long time been skilled in *Fa-hua san-mei*." Here it appears that the meditation is simply a kind of religious practice that one employs in order to be able to understand the true meaning of the *Lotus Sutra*. In chapter 24, which deals with a bodhisattva named Mystic

Sound, it is stated that "he had long ago planted the roots of manifold excellences, had made offerings to and associated familiarly with countless hundreds of thousands of myriads of millions of Buddhas, and had achieved all kinds of profound wisdom." As a result of these efforts, the bodhisattva had attained sixteen types of samadhi, or meditation, among them the *Lotus Sutra* meditation.

Here, it appears that *Lotus Sutra* meditation means the kind of enlightenment or true understanding of reality that comes after one has carried out the religious practices enjoined in the *Lotus Sutra*. As the later T'ien-t'ai master Miao-lo states in one of his commentaries: "The understanding of the True Way in all its aspects is called *Lotus Sutra* meditation."

However, merely by reading the text of the *Lotus Sutra* it is very difficult to understand the meaning of the *Lotus Sutra* meditation or to discover just how such a state is to be attained. Buddhist enlightenment, we must always remember, is not something that can be easily put into words. The fact that the texts of the sutras do not spell out the meaning of enlightenment simply indicates that true understanding lies on a level that transcends verbal expression. As the Buddhist expression has it, enlightenment lies at the place "where words and phrases are cut off and the actions of the mind come to an end." It is none other than the Mystic Law that constitutes the true reality underlying the Buddha nature, the "true entity of all phenomena" and the "unification of the three truths."

The truth, then, is to be found not in the surface or literal level of the *Lotus Sutra,* not in the words themselves, but in a deeper level underlying them. We should not assume from this, however, that one can set aside the Buddhist writings and employ some other means to gain a knowledge of the Buddha. There is no avenue of approach to enlightenment other than through the writings themselves, and through the *Lotus Sutra* in particular.

Miao-lo states in the same commentary mentioned above: "Though enlightenment lies in the realm of present reality, in all cases it is a matter of nursing the original seeds [of enlightenment]." In other words, though all persons who attain enlightenment do so through the means of the *Lotus Sutra,* what they are in effect doing is nourishing and bringing to life the seeds of enlightenment that were planted long ages in the past and which lie beneath the surface of the words of the text. In enlightenment, one does not learn or experience something new, but awakens to a knowledge of something that was already present in one from the beginning.

When Hui-ssu attained an understanding of the *Lotus Sutra* meditation, he suddenly, as a result of his long and arduous studies of the *Lotus Sutra,* was able to perceive these eternal seeds of enlightenment that were hidden within himself and beneath the words of the text.

My teacher Josei Toda often used to speak of "remembering the eternal," by which he meant this power of the individual to recall or reawaken to eternal truths or events that transcend the dimensions of time and space. In *The Human Revolution,* which deals with his life, such an instance is described. It took place during the years of the Second World War when he had been sent to prison by the Japanese military authorities because of his religious convictions. Each day in his prison cell he would chant the *daimoku* and read and recite the text of the *Lotus Sutra,* and as he continued this practice day after day, suddenly he underwent a mystic experience in which he was able to recall how he himself had been present at the gathering on Eagle Peak in India when Shakyamuni Buddha preached the *Lotus Sutra.* Such an experience may be difficult to explain in rational terms, but it is an example of how one may come to perceive the Buddha that is present within one's own being.

In Hui-ssu's later years, when T'ien-t'ai Chih-i, whom we shall discuss in the following chapter, came to study under him, Hui-ssu is reported to have said: "Long ago we were together on Eagle Peak and listened to the *Lotus Sutra.* Now, pursuing those old bonds of karma, you have come again."

These words of Hui-ssu have been interpreted in various ways— as an expression of the respect which Hui-ssu instinctively felt for his new-found disciple, as an encouragement to Chih-i in his studies, or as a gesture of kindliness and affection. But however one interprets them, the fact is that Hui-ssu and Chih-i had both realized in the depths of their being what it means to be among those who listened to the *Lotus Sutra* on Eagle Peak. Proof of this may be found in the famous words which Chih-i himself uttered later in his life: "The gathering on Eagle Peak solemnly continues and has not yet come to an end!"

Before closing this discussion of the significance of the phrase *Lotus Sutra* meditation, I would like to add one last word of explanation so as to avoid any possibility of misunderstanding. We must always keep in mind that, for persons like ourselves living in the present age and attempting to pursue the path of a bodhisattva and carry out the teachings of Buddhism, it is not necessary for us to adopt the precise practices prescribed in Hui-ssu's *Lotus Sutra* meditation or those described in Chih-i's major work, *Great Concentration and Insight* (Ch., *Mo-ho Chih-kuan;* J., *Maka Shikan*). Nor is it necessary for us to endeavor to call up memories of the time when we participated in the gathering at Eagle Peak. In this latter day, Nichiren Daishonin has manifested for us the Gohonzon, which depicts the "gathering on Eagle Peak that has not yet come to an end" and the state of enlightenment that it embodies. Through the act of receiving and diligently praying to the Gohonzon, we may gain a direct and immediate realization of the teachings of Buddhism. And when we have done that, we will in effect become participants in the gathering on Eagle Peak.

Coming Face to Face with the Buddha

Hui-ssu, after he had attained enlightenment and come to realize the true nature of the *Lotus Sutra* meditation, appears to have become a wholly new person. Thereafter he devoted himself with vigorous energy to the propagation of the *Lotus Sutra* and its doctrines. According to his own account, around the age of thirty-four he set off on a journey to the Buddhist centers of the Honan area. There he engaged in doctrinal debates with the members of the religious communities he visited. His views evidently aroused violent opposition, and we are told that he was poisoned by one of the monks who disagreed with his teachings and barely escaped with his life. So fervently did he carry out the injunction of the *Lotus Sutra* to spread its teachings abroad that conflict and persecution became all but inevitable.

Given the conditions that prevailed in the world of Chinese Buddhism at the time, one would naturally expect him to face enmity and opposition. As we have seen in an earlier chapter, the various schools of Buddhism that flourished at this time generally placed either the *Flower Garland Sutra* or the *Nirvana Sutra* in the position of highest honor and relegated the *Lotus Sutra* to the second or third place. Hui-ssu attacked such views head-on, insisting that the *Lotus Sutra* should be accorded the place of greatest honor. His opponents, incensed by his arguments, quite naturally did all they could to make trouble for him.

Hui-ssu wrote about the peaceful practices described in the chapter of the *Lotus Sutra* that bears that name, but the practices he himself carried out were difficult and taxing and involved him in frequent danger. In addition to the attempt on his life mentioned above, his biography mentions several other attempts to poison him at a subsequent period. But Hui-ssu seems to have anticipated such difficulties when he first set out to propagate the teachings of the *Lotus Sutra* and to have resigned himself to them. His rigorous missionary activities, far from being easy or peaceful, remind us of the *shakubuku* practices described in the writings of Nichiren Daishonin.

From this fact too, it is apparent that Hui-ssu's *Lotus Sutra* meditation was not simply a process of quiet meditation or concentration of mind. Rather it demanded of him that he translate the truths of the *Lotus Sutra* that he had come to comprehend into action, following the practices enjoined by the *Lotus Sutra* itself. In this sense, the *Lotus Sutra* meditation that Hui-ssu came to understand when he was around the age of thirty-two represents not only his own personal enlightenment, but a powerful fountain of energy that would in time transform the entire history of Buddhism in China, directing it into wholly new channels.

Earlier I said that Hui-ssu after his enlightenment seemed to become a completely new person. This is hardly surprising. Having studied the various doctrines of the Hinayana and Mahayana teachings, he had, in his *Lotus Sutra* meditation, ascended to what, at least for those of us who are followers of Nichiren Daishonin's Buddhism, represents the highest peak among the teachings of the Buddha, the *Lotus Sutra*. From this eminence, he could look down upon the lesser peaks represented by the other Mahayana sutras and the doctrines of the other schools and could thereafter confront the masters and theoreticians of the time who espoused other doctrines and debate with them with full confidence, certain that his own views were based upon the deepest levels of meaning of the *Lotus Sutra*.

Later in Hui-ssu's life, when he had gone to live on Mount Ta-su in southern Honan in order to escape the harassment of his opponents, a number of disciples gathered around him. Among those who came to study with him was Chih-i, the monk who was later to become known as the Great Teacher T'ien-t'ai. Hui-ssu immediately showed Chih-i the Samantabhadra Practice Hall and explained to him the four types of peaceful practices that were to be carried out there. These are recitation practices based upon chapter 28 of the *Lotus Sutra*, which deals with the bodhisattva Samantabhadra, and meditation practices based on chapter 14, "Peaceful Practices." The fact that Hui-ssu did not hesitate to introduce his new disciple at once to these practices indicates that he had complete confidence in the understanding that he himself had gained in his *Lotus Sutra* meditation.

Chih-i proceeded to carry out these *Lotus Sutra* meditation practices just as Hui-ssu had revealed them to him. After doing so for a period of fourteen days, he suddenly entered into a state of complete concentration in both body and mind and became fully enlightened to the true meaning of the *Lotus Sutra*, just as Hui-ssu had before him. Both Hui-ssu and Chih-i experienced a sudden awakening after their years of study and religious practice, but what exactly was it that they became awakened to? To state it briefly, it was the fact that each person, in this life and just as he or she is, can attain Buddhahood. For those of us who are students of Nichiren Daishonin's Buddhism, this may appear to be a truism. But to most of the people of Hui-ssu's time it must have seemed like a very profound and puzzling concept, one that they experienced difficulty in accepting.

In earlier Buddhism, it had been customary to assume that ordinary human beings cannot hope to attain Buddhahood unless they free themselves entirely from desires and worldly entanglements. In order to do this, they must undergo a long series of difficult religious practices, moving gradually upward stage by stage until they have at last attained the highest level of enlightenment. But Hui-ssu, through his studies of the concept of *shunyata*, or emptiness, as it is expounded in the philosophy of Nagarjuna and through the meditations on emptiness described in the *Treatise on the Large Perfection of Wisdom*, was able to transcend the limitations of dualistic thinking and to realize that ordinary human beings are identical with the Buddha just as they are, that the seeds of delusion are the same as the seeds of enlightenment, that both ordinary beings and Buddhas share the very same nature. This is the level of understanding which we have described as the *Lotus Sutra* meditation, the level expressed in the often-employed phrases "Earthly desires are none other than enlightenment" and "Ignorance is none other than nirvana." Once one has attained this level of understanding, then the possibility of Buddhahood comes clearly into view on the horizon.

It is not surprising, therefore, that in *Great Concentration and Insight* we should so often find Chih-i, Hui-ssu's disciple, speaking of "seeing the Buddha" or "beholding the body of the Buddha." The processes of concentration and insight described in that work are in fact practices by which the individual can transform his own outlook and understanding so that he can perceive the Buddha nature in others and can go out among the populace and effectively help to lead others to enlightenment. The aim of these practices is to assist one to carry out the actions of a bodhisattva, one who is not content to rest in his own enlightenment but who works to lead others to enlightenment as well. In this respect, they differ from the meditation practices that were taught later by the Ch'an

(Japanese, Zen) School of Buddhism, which rejects the authority of the Buddhist scriptures and seeks only the enlightenment of the individual.

Thus, for example, *Great Concentration and Insight* states: "When one carries out the meditation on a single practice, then one will see the various Buddhas right before his eyes and will ascend to the rank of a bodhisattva." In the practices described in the *Lotus Sutra* meditation and *Great Concentration and Insight,* the goal is not merely one's own enlightenment, as in the practices of the Ch'an Sect, but the salvation of all beings. And in order to accomplish this objective, one must of course go out into society and work to propagate the teachings. Only in this way can one carry out the bodhisattva ideal.

The true spirit of Mahayana Buddhism is aptly summed up in the phrase, "Above, to seek enlightenment; below, to spread the teachings to others." On the higher plane, one humbly strives to discover the truth and to reach the understanding of a Buddha, while on the lower plane of everyday life, one goes out among the people of the world, who are floundering in the sea of suffering and ignorance, and does all one can to guide them to salvation. Only when both types of activity are carried out can we say that a person is a true follower of Buddhism. If one forgets this principle and attempts to cut himself off from others and to devote all his effort to his own spiritual improvement alone, then he has wholly misunderstood the basic spirit of the Buddhist teachings.

HUI-SSU AND THE CONCEPT OF THE LATTER DAY OF THE LAW

Hui-ssu remained on Mount Ta-su for a period of eleven years. It was a relatively peaceful era in his life, when many young men, fleeing the troubled political situation of the time, made their way to Mount Ta-su and placed themselves under Hui-ssu's guidance.

It was at this time, when Hui-ssu was forty-four, that he wrote the autobiographical work *Writing Setting Forth My Vow.* The vow which Hui-ssu made at this time was to write out in gilt characters the texts of the *Lotus Sutra* and the *Prajna Sutra*. At the same time that he set forth his vow in writing, he wrote down his reflections on the course of his life.

Hui-ssu's immediate reason for vowing to copy the sutras in gold letters was to pray for the salvation of all the hostile Buddhist scholars and monks who had so vigorously opposed him. As he himself states, he was "moved by a great spirit of compassion" to take this step in hopes of awakening an attitude of religious faith and understanding in his opponents. Like a true bodhisattva, he did not hate those who had sought to poison him or otherwise do him injury, but compassionately worked for their salvation.

Hui-ssu may have been moved to feel particularly compassionate toward his enemies and concerned about their spiritual state because of the view he held regarding the condition of Buddhism in his time. It was widely believed among Mahayana Buddhists that, in the years following the death of Shakyamuni Buddha, the religion which he founded would undergo three distinct phases or periods of development. The first of these is called the period of the Correct Law, also known as the Former Day of the Law. According to some versions of the theory, this period lasts five hundred years, while according to others it extends for a thousand years. During this period, the teachings of Buddhism flourish and enlightenment is relatively easy to attain.

This is followed by the period of the Imitative Law, also called the Middle Day of the Law. Accounts as to its length differ, some describing it as five hundred years in length, others as a thousand. During this period, Buddhism becomes increasingly formalized and progressively fewer people are able to gain enlightenment through its practices. This period gives way to the End of the Law, also known as the Latter Day of the Law, which is said to last for ten thousand years or more. During this period, Buddhism falls into confusion and it becomes extremely difficult for anyone to gain enlightenment.

Obviously, opinions will differ as to exactly when this final period in the development begins, depending upon what view one takes regarding the date of Shakyamuni's death and how long one believes the two earlier periods will last. It is apparent from Hui-ssu's writings, however, that he believed the world had already entered the final phase, the Latter Day of the Law, when the religion is fated to fall on evil times. In *Writing Setting Forth My Vow* he states: "Following the passing of the Buddha, the Correct Law prevailed in the world for a period of five hundred years. After the demise of the Correct Law, the Imitative Law prevailed in the world for a thousand years. Since the demise of the Imitative Law, the End of the Law has come to prevail, and will do so for ten thousand years. I, Hui-ssu, was born in Wu-chin Prefecture, Ju-yang Commandery, in the province of Nan-yü in the state of Wei in the eighty-second year of the Latter Day of the Law, when the countermarker of Jupiter was in the cyclical sign *i-wei* [A.D. 515], on the eleventh day of the eleventh month."

The political and social turmoil that prevailed in Hui-ssu's time must have confirmed his belief that the world had entered the period of the Latter Day of the Law, as must the hostility and abuse that he met with from his adversaries among the Buddhist community. And his determination to copy the *Lotus Sutra* and *Prajna Sutra* in gilt letters and store them away in jeweled boxes, where they would be preserved until the bodhisattva Maitreya, the Buddha of the future, appeared in the world, likewise reflected that belief.

But we should take care to note that his belief that the world had entered a period of religious decay did not lead him into an attitude of despair or fatalism. On the contrary, he seems to have felt that, because of the troubled era he was living in, he had to subject himself to even greater austerities and strive doubly hard to reform the evils of the world and lead others to salvation. And as he cast about for some means to attain enlightenment that would be appropriate for this Latter Day, he became increasingly convinced that the only answer lay in the *Lotus Sutra* and its practices.

Hui-ssu left a number of writings that were of great importance in the development of the T'ien-t'ai Sect. As we have seen, he was critical of the exegetical approach to Buddhism that prevailed in southern China, and instead emphasized the importance of devotion and religious practices. Several of his major works deal extensively with such practices. For him the goal and the core of all Buddhist teaching was not intellectual understanding but the religious experience of enlightenment.

In 568, after his long period of residence on Mount Ta-su, he moved to Nan-yüeh, or Mount Heng in present-day Hunan, where he spent his remaining days. Because of his residence there, he is customarily referred to as Nan-yüeh Hui-ssu. In recognition of his eminence as a religious leader, the emperor of the Ch'en dynasty that ruled southern China from 557 to 589 bestowed upon him the title the Great Teacher of Meditation. He died in 577 at the age of sixty-two.

7. T'ien-t'ai Chih-i and His Three Major Writings

MASTER INTERPRETER OF THE *Lotus Sutra*

I would like to turn now to an examination of the life and thought of Chih-i, Hui-ssu's most outstanding disciple, who is often referred to as the Great Teacher T'ien-t'ai because of his long association with the Buddhist center at Mount T'ien-t'ai in Chekiang Province. Chih-i devoted almost his entire life to the study and elucidation of the *Lotus Sutra* and the principles underlying it, and it is no exaggeration to say that no one in the history of Indian, Chinese, or Japanese Buddhism surpasses him as an authority on that sutra. Reading his biography, one almost has the impression that he was born into the world for the express purpose of expounding the teachings of the *Lotus Sutra* in logical and philosophical terms and systematizing them for the better understanding of believers.

Though his contemporaries did not always agree with his conclusions, they recognized the importance of his labors, and many of them praised him highly. Thus, for example, Chi-tsang (549–623), eminent authority on the San-lun, or Three Treatise, School, praised Chih-i as the kind of masterful figure who appears perhaps once in a thousand years. And if I may add a personal note, I would like to mention that on my recent visit to the People's Republic of China, when I met with Mr. Chao P'u-ch'u of the Buddhist

Association of China, he assured me that in present-day China as well the thought and writings of Chih-i continue to be intensively studied among members of the Buddhist community.

Of course, we must keep in mind that Chih-i lived some fifteen hundred years ago, when conditions in society were very different from what they are now. China in Chih-i's time, particularly southern China, was dominated by the great aristocratic clans, and Buddhism tended to be the monopoly of the aristocracy and the intellectual class. It was not like the popularly centered society and Buddhism of today, and its understanding of the *Lotus Sutra* was accordingly different from ours today.

Nevertheless, the basic principles underlying the *Lotus Sutra,* which constitute the core of Mahayana teaching, remain the same throughout the ages, whether in the time of Chih-i or our present century. They point to the life force or Buddha nature that is shared by all individuals alike, regardless of birth or social position, and call upon the individual to awaken to this nature within him, to develop its unlimited potentialities for wisdom and understanding, and in this way to create for himself a truly happy and fortune-filled life. For us today, the important thing is to ponder these principles set forth three thousand years ago in the *Lotus Sutra,* at times consulting the major writings of Chih-i to aid us in our understanding, and to remain faithful to the unchanging ideals of the Mahayana faith, working at all times to put them into practice in our present age.

But to return to the subject of Chih-i, let us first examine the facts of his life, and then discuss his views regarding the *Lotus Sutra,* particularly as they are set forth in his so-called three major writings, *The Profound Meaning of the Lotus Sutra* (Ch., *Fa-hua Hsüan-i;* J., *Hokke Gengi*), *Words and Phrases of the Lotus Sutra* (Ch., *Fa-hua Wen-chü;* J., *Hokke Mongu*), and *Great Concentration and Insight.*

The principal source for the life of Chih-i is *The Separate Biography of the Great Teacher T'ien-t'ai Chih-che of the Sui* (hereafter referred to as *The Separate Biography*), which was compiled by Chih-i's disciple Kuan-ting (561–632). Also important are the *Kuo-ch'ing Pai-lu,* a collection of documents pertaining to Chih-i's life compiled by Kuan-ting, and the biography of Chih-i in *Further Biographies of Eminent Monks* by Tao-hsüan.

According to these sources, Chih-i was born in Hua-jung in Ching-chou in the region of Lake Tung-t'ing. The year of his birth was probably 538, but since his birth date is calculated backward from the year of his death, and since sources disagree somewhat as to how old he was when he died, other dates are given for his birth. His family name was Ch'en and his father was a government official under the Liang dynasty, which ruled southern China from 502 to 557.

According to *The Separate Biography*, Chih-i's first encounter with the *Lotus Sutra* came at the age of seven—six by Western reckoning—when he visited a temple and heard the monks reciting chapter 25 of the *Lotus Sutra*, the chapter on Kannon, or Avalokiteshvara. The account tells us that the child immediately committed the text to memory on the basis of a single hearing. The incident is meant to indicate the extraordinary intelligence and ability that Chih-i displayed even as a child, but at the same time hints at a mysterious bond that connected him with the *Lotus Sutra*, and with the "Avalokiteshvara" chapter in particular.

From early times, four chapters have been regarded as the four most important sections of the *Lotus Sutra:* chapter 2, the "Skillful Means" chapter; chapter 14, the "Peaceful Practices" chapter; chapter 16, the "Duration of Life" chapter; and this chapter, the "Avalokiteshvara" chapter, which is devoted to a description of the numerous and varied measures that the bodhisattva Avalokiteshvara takes in order to bring salvation to all beings, and constitutes a basic exposition of the bodhisattva ideal.

From the time when Buddhism was introduced to China from India, various sutras and other writings had been expounded to the Chinese by one Buddhist leader or another. But in preaching the saving power of the *Lotus Sutra*, no one was to rival Nan-yüeh Hui-ssu or T'ien-t'ai Chih-i. It must have been a sign of the destiny that lay before him that Chih-i, when still a mere child, responded as he did to the description of the bodhisattva's tireless efforts to bring enlightenment to humankind. Even at this young age, something in his inner being must have awakened to the message of the "Avalokiteshvara" chapter.

As the son of a prominent government official, Chih-i no doubt received the education usual for members of the literati class, a thorough grounding in the Confucian classics and the texts of Taoism, as well as instruction in the reading and writing of poetry and belles-lettres. Indeed, a reading of Chih-i's writings shows clearly that he had a wide acquaintance with secular as well as religious literature and was concerned that his ideas should be expressed in such a way as to be understood not only by members of the Buddhist clergy but by society in general.

Had the times been more peaceful, Chih-i might have followed his father in pursuing a career in government service, or have become a military leader like his elder brother, Ch'en Chen. But the Liang dynasty was beset by rebellion and turmoil, and finally came to an end in 557. Everywhere around him Chih-i could see the dire effects of misrule and social disorder. When shifts in the political situation deprived his family of its former position and power, and death carried off both his parents, Chih-i determined to abandon secular life and enter the Buddhist Order. I like to think that his decision was not motivated simply by grief and despair, however, but by a vision of ideals transcending those of the political and social world of his time, that he was moved to embark upon this new life in hope of gaining an understanding of the principles underlying human existence and thereby helping to relieve the sufferings of others. In any event, despite the pleas of his elder brother, who was now the only member of his immediate family remaining alive, he entered the Buddhist priesthood in 555 at the age of eighteen under Fa-hsü of the Kuo-yüan-ssu temple in Hsiang-chou.

Encounter with Nan-yüeh Hui-ssu

After entering monastic life, Chih-i applied himself to the initial steps of religious training, first under Fa-hsü, then under another monk named Hui-k'uang. Following that, he journeyed to Mount

Ta-hsien in Heng-chou, where he devoted himself to the study of the threefold *Lotus Sutra*, that is, the *Sutra of Infinite Meaning*, which serves as an introduction to the *Lotus Sutra*, the *Lotus Sutra* itself, and its epilogue, the *Sutra of Meditation on Bodhisattva Samantabhadra*. We may surmise that it was around this time that he gradually became convinced of the superiority of the *Lotus Sutra*, assigning it to a position of supreme importance among all the Mahayana sutras.

At the age of twenty-three, Chih-i traveled to Mount Ta-su in southern Honan, where he became a disciple of the famous teacher Nan-yüeh Hui-ssu. As already related in the previous chapter, Hui-ssu was by this time openly proclaiming the superiority of the *Lotus Sutra*, a view that made him the target of attack and abuse among many of the other Buddhist leaders of the time. In fact, he had withdrawn to Mount Ta-su in order to avoid the opposition of his enemies. Despite the difficulties involved, Chih-i sought Hui-ssu out in that remote and war-torn region on the border between southern and northern China, perhaps because he had already learned that Hui-ssu shared his own conviction in the absolute superiority of the *Lotus Sutra*. Certainly he was well aware of Hui-ssu's reputation as a teacher of rare ability and understanding and, knowing how important it is in one's religious studies to place oneself under the guidance of a truly worthy mentor, he braved the dangers of the road and made his way to Mount Ta-su.

As we have already noted in the preceding chapter, Hui-ssu seems to have instinctively recognized the importance of this new disciple, and greeted him with the words, "Long ago we were together on Eagle Peak and listened to the *Lotus Sutra*. Now, pursuing those old bonds of karma, you have come again." He immediately introduced Chih-i to the various kinds of meditation and other religious practices carried out at his establishment. Chih-i, after pursuing these practices for a period of fourteen days, entered into a state of complete concentration and became enlightened to the true meaning of the *Lotus Sutra*, an event that came to be referred to as his enlightenment on Mount Ta-su.

In the course of his earlier studies, Chih-i had attained a degree of illumination when he came to realize that the *Lotus Sutra* deserves to rank first among all the sutras. Under the guidance of Hui-ssu, that earlier enlightenment was now deepened and confirmed in the experience that came to him on Mount Ta-su. At the same time, that experience signified that he had received the sanction of his teacher and that his understanding was now on a level with that of Hui-ssu. The all-important Dharma, or understanding of the truth, had been transmitted from Hui-ssu to Chih-i, and Hui-ssu no doubt rejoiced to think that he had found a disciple who was worthy to receive it.

Chih-i remained on Mount Ta-su for the following seven years, making certain that he had received all that his teacher had to give and that he understood Hui-ssu's doctrines fully and correctly. Then he took leave of the mountain and went to Chin-ling (also called Chien-k'ang), the present-day Nanking, which at this time served as the capital of the Ch'en dynasty, the dynasty that had replaced the Liang in south China in 557.

Residing at a temple called Wa-kuan-ssu, he remained in Chin-ling for eight years, lecturing on the *Lotus Sutra* and other texts and enjoying the patronage of high officials in the Ch'en bureaucracy. At this time he delivered a series of lectures on the title of the *Lotus Sutra* that were later to take shape as *The Profound Meaning of the Lotus Sutra*.

The teachings of this young monk, who was still in his early thirties, aroused considerable controversy and opposition among the Buddhist clergy of the time, since they contradicted the commonly held view of the superiority of the *Nirvana Sutra* and other accepted tenets of southern Buddhism. Chih-i no doubt often found himself engaged in debate with his opponents and called on to defend his ideas in public. At the same time, he attracted many disciples and lay followers.

Despite the outward signs of success, however, Chih-i felt that too few of his followers were able to grasp the true significance of his doctrines, and in the autumn of 575, at the age of thirty-eight, he abruptly left the Wa-kuan-ssu in Chin-ling and journeyed south to Mount T'ien-t'ai (actually, a range of mountains) on the seacoast of Chekiang Province. Mount T'ien-t'ai was noted for its wild and beautiful scenery and from early times had been a center of both Buddhist and Taoist religious activities. In this remote mountain region, Chih-i took up residence.

Sometime after arriving on Mount T'ien-t'ai, Chih-i was carrying out ascetic and meditational practices on Hua-ting Peak, the highest point in the mountain range, when, on a night of violent wind, lightning, and thunder, he underwent a mystical experience. It seemed to him that he was being attacked by demons, but he held firm in his defiance and was rewarded by a vision that confirmed him in the rightness of his beliefs. Like his earlier experiences of enlightenment at Mount Ta-hsien and Mount Ta-su, the event marked a major step in his spiritual development, representing a final proof that the road to understanding that he had been traveling was the correct one and that he should henceforth work to spread his teachings with diligence and compassion, fully assured of their validity.

A few years after retiring to Mount T'ien-t'ai, Chih-i and his band of followers were granted support and financial assistance by Emperor Hsüan of the Ch'en dynasty. Chih-i, distressed at the fishing activities that were carried on along the seacoast at the foot of the mountain and filled with pity for the fishermen whose occupation involved the taking of life, is said to have used part of this financial assistance to buy the fishing rights along the shore and to persuade the local people to give up fishing activities. To us today, such steps may seem puzzling or even pointless. But we must remember that according to Buddhist belief those who engage in occupations that involve the taking of life are creating a fund of bad karma for themselves and putting great obstacles in the way of their salvation. Chih-i's moves to curb such activities represent an attempt to demonstrate in concrete terms the sanctity of life and the need for a more compassionate approach to living, as well as indicating Chih-i's desire to spread the teachings of Buddhism among the populace in general and to assist them on the road to salvation.

Emperor Hsüan's successor to the throne, Hou-chu, the last of the Ch'en-dynasty rulers, made repeated attempts to persuade Chih-i to leave his mountain retreat and return to the capital. At last, after several refusals, Chih-i in 585 responded to the ruler's request and journeyed to Chin-ling. In 587 at the temple called the Kuang-che-ssu he delivered the series of lectures that later were compiled as *Words and Phrases of the Lotus Sutra,* the second of his three major works. It was at this time that he first encountered the young monk Kuan-ting, who later became his foremost disciple and the compiler of his writings and is known to later ages as the Great Teacher Chang-an. Chih-i was fifty at the time and Kuan-ting was twenty-seven.

In the following year, 588, armies from the north swept down in attack on the Ch'en dynasty and Chih-i, to escape the turmoil, fled southwest to Mount Lu and then south to Mount Heng, where his teacher Nan-yüeh Hui-ssu had lived in his closing years. After the overthrow of the Ch'en dynasty in 589, Chih-i returned to Ching-chou, the region of his birth, and founded a temple called the Yü-ch'üan-ssu. There in 593 he expounded the teachings that make up *The Profound Meaning of the Lotus Sutra,* drawing on ideas that he had expounded earlier in his lectures at the Wa-kuan-ssu in Chin-ling. In 594, he expounded the teachings that constitute his third major work, *Great Concentration and Insight.* Eventually he returned to Mount T'ien-t'ai, where he died in 597 at the age of sixty. While he was still alive, Emperor Yang of the newly founded Sui dynasty (589–618) bestowed on him the title Chin-che, or Wise One, and in T'ang times he was posthumously honored with the title T'ien-t'ai Ta-shih or the Great Teacher T'ien-t'ai.

Words and Phrases of the Lotus Sutra

The three major writings of T'ien-t'ai Chih-i hold a place of unparalleled importance in the history of Chinese Buddhism, and indeed in the history of Mahayana Buddhism as a whole. Nichiren Daishōnin, writing of them in his work entitled *Selection of the Time,* says:

"Around the middle of the thousand years of the Middle Day of the Law, the Great Teacher T'ien-t'ai Chih-che appeared. In the ten volumes and thousand leaves of his *Profound Meaning of the Lotus Sutra,* he discussed in detail the meaning of the five characters that make up the title of the *Lotus Sutra, Myoho-renge-kyo.* In the ten volumes of his *Words and Phrases of the Lotus Sutra,* he discussed each word and phrase of the sutra, from the opening words, "Thus have I heard," through the very last words, "they bowed and departed." He interpreted them in the light of four guidelines, namely, causes and circumstances, correlated teachings, the theoretical and the essential teachings, and the observation of the mind, once more devoting a thousand leaves to the discussion.

"In the twenty volumes that make up these two works, *The Profound Meaning of the Lotus Sutra* and the *Words and Phrases of the Lotus Sutra,* he likened the teaching of all the other sutras to streams and rivers and the *Lotus Sutra* to the great ocean. He demonstrated that the waters that make up the Buddhist teachings of all the worlds of the ten directions flow, without loss of a single drop, into that great ocean of the *Myoho-renge-kyo.* In addition, he examined all the doctrines of the great scholars of India, not overlooking a single point, as well as the doctrines of the ten teachers of northern and southern China, refuting those that deserved to be refuted and adopting those that were worthy of acceptance. In addition to the works just mentioned, he also wrote *Great Concentration and Insight* in ten volumes, in which he summed up the Buddha's lifetime teachings on meditation in the concept of *ichinen,* and encompassed all the living entities and their environments of the Ten Worlds in the concept of *sanzen.*

"The pronouncements found in this work of T'ien-t'ai surpass those of all the scholars who lived in India during the thousand years of the Former Day of the Law, and are superior to the commentaries of the teachers who lived in China during the five hundred years preceding T'ien-t'ai."

It is customary in Japan to refer to these three major works of T'ien-t'ai Chih-i as the *Gen* (*Hokke Gengi, The Profound Meaning of the Lotus Sutra*), *Mon* (*Hokke Mongu, Words and Phrases of the Lotus*

Sutra), and *Shikan* (*Maka Shikan, Great Concentration and Insight*), but let us take them in the order in which they were composed and begin our discussion with *Words and Phrases of the Lotus Sutra.*

First we must take up the question of just when and where the lectures that form the basis of the *Words and Phrases* were delivered. Chih-i's disciple Kuan-ting, later known as the Great Teacher Chang-an, who compiled the lectures in their present form, states at the very beginning of the work:

"It is a hard thing for a Buddha to appear in the world, and a hard thing for him to preach. It is hard to transmit and translate what he has preached, and hard to fathom and understand it for oneself. It is hard to have an opportunity to listen to the lectures of a master, and hard to note them all down at once. When I was twenty-seven I listened to and received these lectures at Chin-ling, and when I was sixty-nine I revised and put them into final shape at Tan-ch'iu. I now leave them behind as a gift to the worthy men of later ages, hoping that all alike may achieve the wisdom of a Buddha."

Kuan-ting was born in 561, so that by Chinese reckoning he would have been twenty-seven in 587. Hence we know that Chih-i, who was fifty at the time, delivered these lectures in Chin-ling, the capital of the Ch'en dynasty, in that year, in which he presented a detailed explication of the *Lotus Sutra* word by word and phrase by phrase. We do not know for certain at what temple the lectures were delivered. We do know, however, that Chih-i, after eleven years of seclusion on Mount T'ien-t'ai, had journeyed to Chin-ling at this time and was residing at the temple called Kuang-che-ssu, so we may surmise that the lectures were given there. He may have delivered the lectures at the urging of the young ruler of the Ch'en dynasty, who had in the past repeatedly invited him to come to the capital. But presumably he had been preparing the material for the lectures over a period of many years and felt that, in any event, the time was now ripe for him to present it to the public.

As we have seen from the quotation above, it took Kuan-ting a period of forty-two years to put the lectures into final shape. Presumably he wanted to make absolutely certain that the lectures were presented to posterity in the most authoritative and suitable form. If we may speculate somewhat, we may suppose that Kuan-ting, who was only twenty-seven when he attended the lectures, was at that time not yet capable of comprehending their full significance and had all he could do simply to get the master's words down on paper, without always understanding their purport. However that may be, we cannot but admire Kuan-ting for the care and effort he expended in the recording and polishing of the lectures. If Chih-i had not had a disciple of Kuan-ting's diligence, it is quite possible that none of the lectures that came to constitute his three major writings would have been preserved for later ages.

"It is hard to have an opportunity to listen to the lectures of a master, and hard to note them all down at once," says Kuan-ting, and he was no doubt speaking from personal experience. The year after Chih-i delivered his lectures on the words and phrases of the *Lotus Sutra,* the armies of the conquering Sui dynasty swept down on Chin-ling and both master and disciple were obliged to flee for safety and go separate ways. Kuan-ting later overtook his master at Mount Lu and accompanied him to Ching-chou, where he was present to record the lectures that Chih-i gave there that came to constitute *The Profound Meaning* and *Great Concentration and Insight.*

Kuan-ting, as we have seen, did not produce the final version of *Words and Phrases* until he was sixty-nine, and in a sense we may say that his whole life was devoted to the task of putting the three great works of his master into definitive form so that they could be handed down to future ages. One thinks of how important is the injunction given in the *Lotus Sutra* "to insure the perpetuation of the Law," how necessary it is to make absolutely certain that the truths of the Buddhist doctrine are correctly transmitted to posterity. At the same time, one contemplates with admiration the manner in which this particular master and disciple, Chih-i and Kuan-ting, worked in perfect harmony to accomplish that purpose.

The content of *Words and Phrases* has already been touched on in the quotation from Nichiren Daishonin above. The work is an exhaustive commentary on the Chinese translation of the *Lotus*

Sutra completed by Kumarajiva in 406. Each of its ten chapters is divided into two parts. Taking up the various terms and phrases of the sutra, Chih-i interprets them in the light of four guidelines: (1) causes and circumstances, or the four ways of preaching which differ according to the circumstances of the expounder and his listeners; (2) correlated teachings, or the four different types of preaching; (3) the theoretical and the essential teachings; and (4) *kanjin,* or the perception of the truth through the observation of the mind.

In addition, *Words and Phrases* is extremely important because of the manner in which Chih-i divides up the contents of the *Lotus Sutra.* First of all, he divides the entire *Lotus Sutra* into three parts, which he labels preparation, revelation, and transmission. The first chapter of the sutra, the "Introduction," represents the section called preparation and sets the stage for what will follow. The next fifteen and a half chapters, from the second chapter through the first half of the seventeenth chapter, constitute revelation and embody the truths that the Buddha imparts to his listeners. The remaining eleven and a half chapters of the sutra, from the latter half of the seventeenth chapter through the twenty-eighth chapter, represents transmission, in which the Buddha urges that his doctrines be diligently handed down to later ages.

At the same time, Chih-i divides the *Lotus Sutra* into two parts: the theoretical teachings, represented by the first fourteen chapters of the sutra, and the essential teachings, represented by the remaining fourteen chapters. He also applies the three divisions of preparation, revelation, and transmission to both the theoretical and essential teachings in turn. Thus, within the theoretical teachings, the "Introduction" chapter represents preparation, the eight chapters from the second chapter through the ninth chapter represent revelation, and the five chapters from the tenth chapter through the fourteenth chapter represent transmission. In the case of the essential teachings, the first half of the fifteenth chapter represents preparation, the one chapter and two halves comprising the latter half of the fifteenth chapter, the entire sixteenth chapter, and the first half of the seventeenth chapter, represent revelation, and the eleven and a half chapters that make up the rest of the sutra constitute transmission.

To fully understand just how this system of classification works out, one would of course have to turn directly to *Words and Phrases* itself. The important thing to note here, however, is that it brings order and systemization to the contents of the *Lotus Sutra* and focuses attention on the sections that, at least in Chih-i's eyes, are of most vital significance. Up to Chih-i's time there had been a vast number of commentaries written on the *Lotus Sutra*, but none had succeeded in elucidating the basic message of the sutra with such clarity and conviction as did these lectures of Chih-i. In the technical language of *Great Concentration and Insight*, he achieved a state of insight known as *nei-chien leng-jan*, or *naigan reinen*, a calm, impartial understanding that reflects the truth with all the fidelity of a fine mirror. It is not surprising that Chih-i's interpretations of the sutra quickly replaced in authority the earlier interpretations of the monk Fa-yün, who had also lectured at the Kuang-che-ssu in Chin-ling, and came to be recognized as the final word on the meaning of the *Lotus Sutra*.

The Profound Meaning of the Lotus Sutra

In the case of *The Profound Meaning of the Lotus Sutra*, a work in ten chapters also compiled by Chih-i's disciple Kuan-ting, no indication of just when Chih-i delivered the lectures upon which it is based can be found in the work. But a much later work on the history of Buddhism, *The Record of the Lineage of the Buddha and the Patriarchs*, which was completed in 1269, states that Chih-i expounded *The Profound Meaning* at the Yü-ch'üan-ssu in Ching-chou in the fourth month of 593, and hence this is the date customarily assigned to the work.

In it, Chih-i discusses the five characters that make up the title of the *Lotus Sutra* in the light of five major principles, which he defines as name, entity, quality, function, and teachings. He goes on to assert that these five principles can be applied in the interpretation of any passage in the sutra.

It may be noted that in the Buddhism of Chih-i, the two concerns of study and practice, scriptural interpretation and devotional exercise, stand side by side like the two wings of a bird or the two wheels of a cart. Neither can be dispensed with, and equal attention must be given to both. The two works by Chih-i we have noted so far are taken up with the former concern, the interpretation of the text of the *Lotus Sutra* and the principles expounded in it. It was not until his final major work, *Great Concentration and Insight,* that Chih-i fully expounded his views on the subject of devotional practice.

But before we leave this discussion of Chih-i's writings on scriptural interpretation, we must note another important doctrine that is set forth in *The Profound Meaning,* that known as "the five periods and the eight doctrines." The Chinese of this period, as we have seen, were much concerned with the problem of how to reconcile the seemingly contradictory teachings presented in the various sutras and how to determine which sutras or teachings deserved to be accorded the highest honor. Chih-i's answer to this question is the brilliant and highly detailed system of classification represented by this doctrine of the five periods and the eight teachings.

This system first of all classifies all the sutras into five chronological periods on the basis of the time when they were believed to have been preached by the Buddha. The first period is represented by the *Flower Garland Sutra.* This sutra was traditionally believed to have been preached shortly after the Buddha first attained enlightenment at Buddh Gaya. Its abstruse metaphysical doctrines proved far too difficult for the Buddha's listeners, however, and left them merely baffled. In the succeeding period, therefore, he preached the much simpler and more elementary truths contained in the Hinayana sutras called the Agamas in the northern tradition of Buddhism. This period is hence known as the Agama period. In contrast to the *Flower Garland Sutra* period, which lasted only three weeks, the Agama period lasted twelve years.

In the third period, the Vaipulya period, he taught doctrines that were broader in application and stressed the equality of the Buddha and the common individual, hence the Chinese translation of Vaipulya, *Fang-teng,* which means "broad and equal." This period lasted eight years and represents an elementary stage in the introduction of Mahayana teachings.

The fourth period lasted twenty-two years, and in it the Buddha taught the metaphysical principles expounded in the Prajna, or Wisdom, sutras. These expound the principle of emptiness (*shunyata*), which stresses that the absolute is without attributes and cannot be defined in words.

The fifth and final period, which embraces the last eight years of the Buddha's life, is represented by the preaching of the *Lotus Sutra* and the *Nirvana Sutra* and constitutes the peak and culmination of his preaching.

This classification of the five periods is Chih-i's answer to other schools of Buddhism which place the *Flower Garland Sutra* or some other Mahayana sutra in the position of prime importance and relegate the *Lotus Sutra* to an inferior position. The five periods came to constitute a fundamental doctrine of the T'ien-t'ai Sect in China and its Japanese counterpart, the Tendai Sect.

The system known as the eight doctrines classifies the teachings of the Buddha not on the basis of chronological periods but on the basis of the methods of teaching used and the content of the teaching. The classification according to method distinguishes four categories. First is the method of abrupt or sudden doctrine, in which the Buddha preaches his message without any preparatory instruction, yet his listeners, because of their superior capacity, are able to grasp the truth. Second is the gradual doctrine, which leads the listeners step by step from less advanced teachings to more difficult ones. Third is the secret doctrine, which the Buddha contrived to preach so that his listeners each benefited from the teachings differently according to their respective capacities without being aware of this. Fourth is the indeterminate doctrine, which different individuals in the audience understand differently. These four categories stress the fact that the Buddha adapted his message to the varied capacities of his listeners and was capable of speaking differently to different individuals at the same time.

The other fourfold classification which makes up the system of the eight doctrines deals with the content of the teachings. The first category is the Hinayana teachings. Second are the connecting teachings, which are common to both Hinayana and elementary Mahayana. Third are the special teachings, which are preached especially for bodhisattvas. Fourth are the round or perfect teachings, which teach the unification of the three truths or the truth of the Middle Way. In this system of classification, as in that of the five periods, the last category represents the highest expression of the truth.

This system of classification of the Buddha's teachings and methods of presentation, as we have stated earlier, represents one of the most complex and impressive achievements in the history of Chinese Buddhist thought. But the two major works of Chih-i we have examined so far, *Words and Phrases* and *The Profound Meaning,* for all their doctrinal importance, do not reveal the full extent and significance of Chih-i's philosophy. It was only with the exposition of the principle of "three thousand worlds in a single instant of thought" that his teachings reached their final form. For an explanation of that principle, we must turn to the last of his major works.

Great Concentration and Insight

There is no doubt as to where or when *Great Concentration and Insight,* the last and most important of Chih-i's three major works, was expounded. The very opening of the work states that the lectures were begun on the twenty-sixth day of the fourth month of 594, the first month of summer, at the Yü-ch'üan-ssu in Ching-chou and continued throughout the summer. Chih-i was fifty-seven at this time and Kuan-ting, who recorded the lectures, was thirty-four. Kuan-ting went over the material a number of times and in the years after Chih-i's death put it into final form. The work is in ten chapters.

The temple called Yü-ch'üan-ssu, whose name means Temple of the Jade Fountain, was said to have been named for a spring of particularly clear and limpid water that flowed out of the ground at that spot, and was no doubt situated in a beautiful mountain setting. According to the records of the event, over a thousand monks gathered to attend these lectures of Chih-i, and three hundred of them received instruction in the meditation practices expounded in them.

As stated earlier, the most important philosophical concept set forth in *Great Concentration and Insight* is that of three thousand worlds in a single instant of thought. This concept, which Chih-i evolved on the basis of teachings in the *Lotus Sutra,* represents an attempt to explain the mutually inclusive relationship of the ultimate truth and the phenomenal world, of the absolute and the relative.

Earlier Buddhist thought had described the Ten Worlds, or ten realms into which beings may be reborn depending upon the kind of karma they have accumulated in their past existences. These realms range from the lowest states of being, such as Hell or the realm of hungry demons, to the highest states, those of the bodhisattva and the Buddha. Earlier Buddhism had seen these states as mutually exclusive—that is, the individual could occupy only one state in a lifetime, and moved from one state to another after the conclusion of that lifetime. In Chih-i's system of thought, the Ten Worlds are multiplied by various factors that condition them to produce a total of three thousand possible worlds, that is, three thousand conditions according to which life may manifest itself. Chih-i then goes on to state that all of these three thousand possible worlds are present within each instant or "life moment" of the individual. Within a single lifetime the individual is capable of moving back and forth any number of times from one realm to another. Thus one may move upward through religious practice and striving until he has reached the ultimate goal, the state of

Buddhahood, without going through a lengthy series of rebirths. Or, conversely, he may, because of evil deeds or neglect of spiritual concerns, move downward in the scale toward the lower realms of existence.

This concept explains why it is possible for one to attain Buddhahood in this present lifetime without having to go through countless existences of arduous spiritual striving, as had been asserted in earlier Buddhism. At the same time, however, it also implies that enlightenment, once attained, is not necessarily a permanent condition, but must constantly be supported and actively sustained if one is not to sink back to a lower level of existence.

In Chih-i's system, the method by which these efforts to improve or sustain one's spiritual advancement are the religious practices referred to in the title *Great Concentration and Insight*. The word "concentration" means to fix one's thoughts on the realm of truth, while "insight" means to realize that truth within one's own mind.

The seventh chapter of *Great Concentration and Insight*, entitled "The Correct Practice," is regarded as the core of the work and sets forth in detail the practice of concentration and insight. According to this chapter, there are ten objects of meditation and ten types of meditation that, when correctly observed, lead one to an understanding and realization of the truth of three thousand worlds in a single instant of thought. The ten objects of meditation are: (1) the phenomenal world, (2) earthly desires, (3) sickness, (4) karmic effect, (5) diabolical functions, (6) attachment to a certain level of meditation, (7) distorted views, (8) arrogance, (9) attachment to the levels of existence represented by learning and realization, and (10) attachment to the level of the bodhisattva.

The ten types of meditation are: (1) meditation on the region of the unfathomable; (2) meditation to arouse compassion; (3) meditation to enjoy security in the realm of truth; (4) meditation to eliminate attachments; (5) meditation to discern what leads to the realization of the true entity of life and what prevents it; (6) meditation to make proper use of the elements conducive to enlightenment (7) meditation to remove obstacles to enlightenment; (8) meditation to recognize the stage of one's progress; (9) meditation to stabilize one's mind and one's progress; and (10) meditation to remove the last barrier to enlightenment. These ten types of meditation are systematically directed to each of the ten objects of meditation in turn in order to achieve a condition of perfect enlightenment.

Chih-i began at a very early age to take an intense interest in the *Lotus Sutra* and its message of salvation. During the long years of study and practice that followed, he worked tirelessly to deepen and broaden his understanding of its principles and to make them accessible to the people of China, laboring to plant the seeds of the truth wherever he traveled or resided. These long years of effort reached their culmination in *Great Concentration and Insight,* which not only sets forth what to Chih-i was the underlying truth expounded in the *Lotus Sutra,* but presents a highly systematized program of spiritual practices by which the devotee may advance step by step in his understanding of that truth until he reaches the final level of enlightenment, that of Buddhahood. It stands as a fitting monument to a lifetime of effort devoted to the elucidation and propagation of the *Lotus Sutra.*

8. Hsüan-tsang and
His Journey to India

T'ANG CULTURE AND HSÜAN-TSANG'S PLACE IN IT

As we have seen in the previous chapter, Chih-i, the Great Teacher T'ien-t'ai, lived into the first years of the Sui dynasty. The Sui carried out the important task of unifying China after several centuries of division and internal strife, but its own rule proved to be short-lived. In 618 it was overthrown and replaced by the T'ang dynasty (618–907), one of the most outstanding eras of traditional Chinese culture. It also marks the golden age of Buddhism in China, a period when the religion reached heights of power and popularity it had not known previously and was never to know again.

The T'ang dynasty has been noted in particular for the cosmopolitan nature of its culture. Embassies from the countries surrounding China such as Japan and Korea and the states of south and central Asia journeyed to the T'ang capital at Ch'ang-an, and the influence of T'ang culture extended in all directions. Foreigners even found their way into the ranks of the Chinese bureaucracy, as in the case of Abe no Nakamaro (701–70), a Japanese who went to China as a student in his youth and remained to become an important official in the T'ang government.

Cosmopolitanism was likewise a keynote in the career of one of the leading Buddhist figures of the period, the monk Hsüan-tsang

(602–64). Like Fa-hsien some centuries earlier, he is known first of all for the extended journey that he made to the states of Central Asia and India, and in particular for the comprehensive account he wrote of his travels, *Records of the Western Region in the Time of the Great T'ang,* a work that has proved to be of inestimable value to scholars of later ages.

Hsüan-tsang was not a follower of the teachings of Chih-i, but was associated with the Wei-shih, or Consciousness-only, School, based on the Yogachara or Vijnanavada teachings of India. In Japan Hsüan-tsang is honored as the founder of the Hosso School, the Japanese counterpart of the Consciousness-only School. For those of us who are adherents of Nichiren Daishonin's Buddhism, he thus stands somewhat outside the main focus of interest. Nevertheless, the zeal which he displayed in setting off on his long and arduous journey in search of a fuller understanding of Buddhism is a source of inspiration for all followers of the faith. In addition, his exploits so captured the imagination of the Chinese people that his story, in highly fictionalized form, became the core of the lengthy romance entitled *Hsi-yu Chi, Journey to the West,* which retains its popularity even today. He is thus one of the most widely known of all Chinese Buddhist figures.

BACKGROUND AND MOTIVES FOR
THE JOURNEY TO INDIA

The principal source for the life of Hsüan-tsang is a work compiled by Hsüan-tsang's disciple Yen-ts'ung (dates unknown) on the basis of an earlier work by Hui-li (c. 615–76). This work, *Ta T'ang Ta-tz'u-en-ssu San-tsang Fa-shih Chuan,* tells us that when Hsüan-tsang was born his mother dreamed that she saw her newborn son dressed in white robes and setting off in a westerly direction. "You are my son!" she exclaimed. "Where are you going?" To which Hsüan-tsang replied, "I am going off in search of the Law."

Of course, anecdotes of this type are common enough in the biographies of eminent Buddhist figures. And in view of the great fame and favor that Hsüan-tsang enjoyed in his later years, it is hardly surprising that his biographers should have wished to emphasize the illustrious career that lay in store for the newborn child by the inclusion of such an anecdote. Yen-ts'ung, as a disciple of Hsüan-tsang, must often have heard his master speak about the motives that led him to embark upon his renowned journey to India, and he was perhaps aware that those motives reached back to the very early years of Hsüan-tsang's childhood.

Hsüan-tsang's youthful years correspond to the period of the founding of the T'ang, a time of political turmoil and foreign expansion. Hsüan-tsang and his older brother Ch'ang-chieh both entered religious life at an early age and, leaving the Lo-yang area where they were born, journeyed to Ch'ang-an and then farther west to Ch'eng-tu in present-day Szechwan Province. From there Hsüan-tsang proceeded on his own to Ching-chou, where the Great Teacher T'ien-t'ai had for a time lived and taught, then to Hsiang-chou in Honan, and finally to Chao-chou in Hopei. In all of these moves, he was searching for a worthy teacher. But it would appear that there was no one in the Buddhist circles of China at that time who was capable of resolving his doubts and giving him the kind of instruction he desired.

Earlier, Hsüan-tsang and his older brother had remained in Ch'ang-an for a period of four years. By this time Hsüan-tsang had reached the age of twenty and had been formally ordained, and we are told that both brothers had attained fame for their religious zeal. Ch'ang-chieh seems to have been the scholarly type and devoted himself to the writings of Confucianism and Taoism as well as to the study of Buddhist texts. By contrast, Hsüan-tsang was much more of an activist, and his restlessness impelled him to keep on traveling around the country in search of a teacher.

After the two brothers had made their way to Ch'eng-tu, Ch'ang-chieh settled down there and in time won wide admiration from the people of the region for his breadth of learning and pursuit of the religious life. He exemplifies one important personality type and manner of living. His younger brother, however, could never be content with such a sedentary existence. He brushed aside the restraints of his older brother and in time was led to embark on a journey that, technically at least, violated the laws of the Chinese empire.

In the course of his studies under various teachers in China, Hsüan-tsang applied himself to the vinaya, or rules of monastic discipline, as well as to the study of various treatises such as the *Abhidharmakosha* and the *Treatise on the Establishment of Truth.* However, he was troubled by the differences of opinion evidenced by these various works and came to feel that his perplexities could be solved only by a journey to the homeland of the Buddhist religion.

One of his particular aims in undertaking the trip to India was to obtain a complete copy of the work known as the *Yogachara-bhumi,* or *Stages of Yoga Practice.* As I have described in my earlier volume on Indian Buddhism, legend asserts that the great fifth-century Buddhist scholar Asanga miraculously ascended to the Tushita Heaven, abode of the mythical bodhisattva Maitreya, and received the text of the *Stages* and other works from the bodhisattva. Scholars now surmise that in fact Asanga received these works from a historical person, presumably his teacher, who happened to bear the name Maitreya. However that may be, Asanga's *Stages of Yoga Practice* was brought to China in the sixth century and translated by the Indian monk Paramartha (499–569), but the translation represented only a part of the original work. Hsüan-tsang's aim was to secure a complete version of the work. He was successful in his quest, returning to China with a complete text which he translated into Chinese, producing the one-hundred-chapter version of the work that is now current.

Of course, this was not Hsüan-tsang's only motive in undertaking the trip to India. He believed, like Fa-hsien before him, that only by going in person to the birthplace of Buddhism could he gain a complete and accurate knowledge of the Mahayana teachings, without which he could not hope to bring true salvation to his fellow human beings.

TO THE CROSSROADS OF CIVILIZATION

Filled with a burning determination to travel to India in search of
the Law, Hsüan-tsang left Ch'ang-an in the fall, in the eighth
lunar month of the third year of the Chen-kuan era, which corresponds to 629 of the Western calendar. Some scholars would date
his departure to 627, when Hsüan-tsang was twenty-six, but here
we will follow the account given by his disciple Yen-ts'ung.

Earlier, Hsüan-tsang and several companions had submitted
papers to the T'ang government requesting official permission to
leave China and journey to the west. At this time, Chinese citizens
were permitted to travel only as far west as Yü-men-kuan, the Jade
Gate Barrier, a checkpoint on the road to the west in present-day
Kansu Province. According to T'ang law, no Chinese was allowed
to go beyond the barrier without special permission from the government. The request for such permission submitted by Hsüan-
tsang and his companions was summarily rejected by the government, and the other members of the group abandoned the idea of
trying to make the journey. Hsüan-tsang, not so easily discouraged,
submitted a second request, but this too was denied approval. He
then made up his mind that, if necessary, he would defy the law of
the land in order to carry out his dream of journeying to India.

It was a very serious decision. And yet, when a man is determined
to pursue a lofty ideal, he must be prepared to take all kinds of
risks. We can judge the quality of Hsüan-tsang's faith and dedication by the fact that he was willing to contemplate such a drastic
step. In the the much fictionalized account in *Journey to the West,*
the T'ang ruler Emperor T'ai-tsung summons Hsüan-tsang into his
presence, presents him with a passport that will see him through the
barrier gate and gifts and companions to accompany him, and even
escorts him part of the way. In actual fact, however, Hsüan-tsang's
departure from Ch'ang-an was a stealthy affair carried out wholly
without the emperor's knowledge or approval.

Having left Ch'ang-an, Hsüan-tsang made his way west as far as
Ch'in-chou in the company of another monk named Hsiao-ta. From
there to Lan-chou and Liang-chou he kept company with other

travelers on the road and the grooms who were escorting trains of government horses. At Liang-chou, where his presence was detected, he was called in by the military governor and ordered to return to Ch'ang-an at once. Hsüan-tsang, however, succeeded in evading surveillance and pushed westward as far as Kua-chou, the region of the Jade Gate Barrier. By this time an order had been sent out for his arrest, but through the kindness of the officials in the region, he was able to slip through the barrier gate under cover of night and make his way out into the desert.

Having successfully evaded the watchful eyes of the T'ang government and accomplished his escape from the country, he now faced the countless days of thirst, hunger, and hardship of a passage across the desert. "The dangers and perils were a hundredfold, a thousandfold too numerous to describe in detail," says the account of his progress. Since we have already fully described the hardships that faced travelers in this region in our earlier chapter on Fa-hsien, we will not repeat those descriptions here, but simply outline the itinerary of Hsüan-tsang's pilgrimage.

Having passed through I-wu, or Hami, the easternmost of the states of Central Asia, he proceeded to Turfan, where the ruler, an ardent follower of Buddhism, treated him with great favor. We are told that there were several thousand Buddhist monks in the state. When Hsüan-tsang lectured on the *Prajnaparamita Sutra of the Benevolent King,* one of the Wisdom sutras that deals with a benevolent king who protects his country, the ruler of Turfan, along with his high ministers and the eminent monks of the state, all gathered to listen. As a special mark of respect, we are told, the king in person crouched down on the floor and offered his back so that Hsüan-tsang could step upon it as he ascended the lecture platform.

As is evident from the *Records of the Western Region in the Time of the Great T'ang,* Hsüan-tsang's own account of his journey, Buddhism flourished in these oasis-kingdoms of Central Asia. Once the ruler of these small communal societies with their relatively limited populations had converted to the Buddhist religion, the entire population of his state proceeded to do likewise.

After leaving Turfan, Hsüan-tsang proceeded to Agni and then to Kucha. Both peoples used writing systems allied to that of India and could read the Indian scriptures in the original languages, and we may assume that the institutions and policies of their states were founded on the principles of the Buddhist teachings. Kucha is the state in which Kumarajiva had been born some three hundred years earlier. As befitted a flourishing area of Buddhist activity, a statue of the Buddha adorned the gate of the capital, and when Hsüan-tsang arrived he was greeted by a musical performance held in his honor.

From there he entered the region of western Turkestan, an area which is now part of the Soviet Union, passed over the highlands of Central Asia and the Syr-Dar'ya River, and arrived at Samarkand. Here almost the entire population, from the ruler down to the ordinary citizens, were followers of the Zoroastrian religion, though there were two Buddhist temples in the state.

Hsüan-tsang's route now turned south, passing through the so-called Iron Gate and crossing the Amu-Dar'ya river into Bactria in the region that is today Afghanistan. This is the area where the Yüeh-chih state—one of the states that Kumarajiva visited as a young man—had flourished in the past, and the area has aptly been called the crossroads of civilization. Here Hsüan-tsang prepared to make the journey over the snowy wastes of the Hindu Kush.

The deep valleys that threaded among the towering peaks of the Hindu Kush range were clogged with snow even in summer and the trails were beset by robbers. Pushing forward through this perilous region for some six hundred *li* (a traditional Chinese unit of measure, about six hundred meters) or more, Hsüan-tsang reached the state of Bamiyan. According to Hsüan-tsang's account in the *Records of the Western Region*, this country measured some two thousand *li* or more east to west and three hundred *li* or more north to south and was situated among the mountains. The state boasted thirty or forty Buddhist temples and several thousand monks. The ruler came out in person to greet Hsüan-tsang and lead him into the palace. What particularly attracted Hsüan-tsang's attention was a colossal image of the Buddha carved in a face of the mountain northwest of the capital, which measured some 140 or 150 Chinese feet in height and was covered with a dazzling coat of gilt.

Hsüan-tsang was fortunate in viewing the statue when it was still unmarred. Later, in the eighth and ninth centuries, when Islamic forces invaded the region, they destroyed the face of the statue and left it in the pitifully mutilated state in which it exists today. Still later, in the thirteenth century, Chinggis Khan led his Mongol armies through the area and wiped out every trace of the capital city of Bamiyan, so that the region came to be referred to as the valley of the dead or the city of ghosts.

Leaving Bamiyan, Hsüan-tsang traversed the remainder of the Hindu Kush and approached northern India. Proceeding by way of Kapisha and Gandhara, he crossed the Indus River and headed toward the central and eastern areas of India.

Gandhara in the past had been a thriving center of the Buddhist religion, and under the patronage of King Kanishka and his successors had produced the highly realistic works of Buddhist sculpture for which it is now famous, works that show a strong Greco-Roman influence. But by the time Hsüan-tsang arrived in the area, its thousand or more Buddhist temples had fallen into decay and its pagodas lay toppled. Considering that Gandhara had been the birthplace of the eminent Buddhist philosophers Asanga and Vasubandhu and the place where the famous Sarvastivadin monk Parshva, acting under the patronage of King Kanishka, had worked to codify the Buddhist scriptures, it must have been a great blow to Hsüan-tsang to find it in such condition.

The fact was that by Hsüan-tsang's time Buddhism in India was in a state of unmistakable decline. Though it was still in a flourishing condition in the states of Central Asia through which he had passed, when Hsüan-tsang reached India, the goal of his journey and the center of his hopes, he found in one locale after another that only remnants of the Buddhist religion were to be encountered. For anyone who was aware of what great prosperity and influence the religion had earlier enjoyed in India, it must have been a cause of great sorrow. As a matter of fact, later in his journey, when

Hsüan-tsang reached the state of Magadha and stood under the pipal tree at Buddh Gaya, the spot where Shakyamuni was believed to have attained enlightenment, we are told that he flung himself on the ground and gave way to lamentation. According to Yen-ts'ung's account, at that time Hsüan-tsang cried out, "What kind of existence was I living at the time when the Buddha attained enlightenment? Now, in the Middle Day of the Law, I have traveled ten thousand miles to make my way here. Why am I so weighed down by the bonds of evil karma?" As Hsüan-tsang wept and grieved in this way over the decay into which the Buddha's teachings had fallen, it is said that many among the several thousand monks who had gathered from far and near in order to spend the summer period of retirement at the spot wept in sympathy with him.

In time Hsüan-tsang visited the famous monastery of Nalanda, which was situated in the northern suburbs of Rajagaha, the capital of Magadha. There he was received with great courtesy and remained for a considerable time. Counting both permanent residents and visitors, Nalanda housed several thousand monks, who concentrated mainly on the study of Mahayana doctrines. It was the largest Buddhist monastery in India at this time and in addition to studies of the various sects of Mahayana and Hinayana Buddhism it offered instruction in the Vedic literature of ancient India as well as in logic, music, medicine, and mathematics. Daily lectures were held at over a hundred sites on the monastery grounds, and the monks in residence were renowned for their devotion to learning.

By the time Hsüan-tsang arrived there, the monastery was already over seven hundred years old, approximately the same age that Oxford and Cambridge are today. The great universities of Europe, one will recall, were originally founded as institutions for the study of theology, though over the course of the centuries theological studies have ceased to hold the place of importance in the curriculum that they once held. Nalanda, on the other hand, had continued from the time of its founding to concentrate its energies upon the study of Buddhist doctrine, a reminder of how profound and complex are the ramifications of Buddhist philosophy. Nalanda was in fact a kind of Buddhist university and one of the greatest repositories of learning in India at the time.

At Nalanda, Hsüan-tsang received instruction from Shilabhadra, the abbot of the monastery and one of the most outstanding scholars of the time, who was said to have been one hundred and six years old when Hsüan-tsang arrived. From Shilabhadra, Hsüan-tsang received instruction in the works of Nagarjuna, Asanga, and Vasubandhu, and in particular in the *Stages of Yoga Practice* and other works of the Consciousness-only School of Buddhism. At the same time, Hsüan-tsang devoted himself to the study of ancient Sanskrit and the languages of the Buddhist scriptures, as well as logic, music, and other subjects, and read a large number of works in Sanskrit. Hsüan-tsang was in his thirties at this time, an ideal age for the pursuit of learning, and we may be certain that in the course of his studies he gained a profound understanding of the principles of Buddhist philosophy. Before he knew it, five years had passed since his arrival at Nalanda.

He then set out on his travels once more, journeying east and then south along the coast of the Indian subcontinent. He intended to cross over to the island state of Ceylon, or Sri Lanka, but civil strife on the island forced him to abandon this plan. He then traveled west to the Arabian Sea coast of western India, crossed the lower reaches of the Indus River, and headed north for the trek back to China.

Earlier, when he had passed through the state of Kamarupa in northeastern India, he had apparently contemplated trying to make his way back to China by the road leading through Tibet to the Chinese province of Szechwan, but he was advised that the route was extremely dangerous and beset with poisonous snakes and other perils, and he consequently abandoned the idea. Instead, from western India he once more crossed over the Hindu Kush, pushed his way over the plateau of the Pamirs and, this time taking the southern route through Central Asia, at last arrived back in Ch'ang-an.

The usual date given for his arrival in the capital is the twenty-fourth day of the first month of Chen-kuan nineteen, or 645; it is said that his journey had occupied a total of seventeen years and that he was forty-four at the time of his return to China. Some scholars, however, maintain that he arrived on the seventh day of the first month of 645 and that he was forty-six at the time, while others assert that his journey had in fact occupied a total of nineteen years.

Whichever version may be correct, there is no question but that it had been a long and extremely difficult trip, as well as a very rewarding one, and no doubt the memories of it remained with Hsüan-tsang as a precious treasure for the rest of his life. His main purpose in making the strenuous journey had been to secure copies of Buddhist texts, and he fulfilled that purpose admirably by returning to China with more than 650 Buddhist texts packed in some 520 cases. The remaining twenty years of his life until his death in 664 were devoted to the task of translating important items among the works he had brought back.

The Beginning of the Sectarian Period

Earlier, we have referred to the scheme set forward by Kogaku Fuse for the periodization of the history of Chinese Buddhism, in which Professor Fuse suggests a five-part division. The fourth period in his scheme, that known as the period of the sects of Buddhism or the sectarian period, begins with Hsüan-tsang's return to Ch'ang-an in 645. In Professor Fuse's view, Hsüan-tsang's return to China was an event of particular significance. Previous to that time, though there had been various schools of Buddhism in China, as we have seen, there had not been a clear consciousness of separate sects within the Buddhist religion. According to Professor Fuse, it was Hsüan-tsang who was mainly instrumental in introducing that kind of sectarian consciousness into the world of Chinese Buddhism.

As we have noted previously, Hsüan-tsang in later times came to be looked on as the founder of the Hosso Sect, the Japanese version of the Consciousness-only Sect of Buddhism. Even during his lifetime he undoubtedly exercised a great influence over the Buddhist world, though whether he was actually responsible for the introduction of rigidly sectarian ways of thought is perhaps questionable. One indication of the importance of his place in Buddhist history is the fact that the translations of Buddhist scriptures that had been made before his time came to be referred to as the old translations, while the translations which he himself made and presented to the T'ang emperor were known as the New Translations. In this sense, his activities without doubt represent the beginning of a new era in the development of Chinese Buddhism.

Because of the fame gained as a result of his lengthy pilgrimage to India and the great favor that he enjoyed with Emperor T'ai-tsung after his return to China, Hsüan-tsang certainly occupied a position of unrivaled eminence in the flourishing world of T'ang-period Buddhism. In spite of such eminence, or perhaps because of it, opinion among Buddhists of later ages regarding his worth has been divided into two opposing camps. Part of the controversy surrounding Hsüan-tsang is based on his New Translations—in some cases retranslations of works that had already been translated into Chinese in earlier periods. There is no doubt that Hsüan-tsang's New Translations are sometimes superior in quality. But it would be wrong to suppose that all the New Translations are necessarily better than the Old Translations. Many scholars hold that in fact the earlier translations done by men such as Kumarajiva or Paramartha are superior to those produced by Hsüan-tsang.

Moreover, the teachings that Hsüan-tsang espoused represent a doctrinal regression in the overall development of Buddhism in China. One of Hsüan-tsang's objectives in going to India was to gain a more thorough knowledge of the teachings of Asanga and Vasubandhu, particularly their expositions of the Consciousness-only teachings. After Hsüan-tsang returned from India, however, he seems to have been less interested in expounding the Consciousness-only teachings as they were interpreted by Asanga and Vasubandhu than in following the version of those teachings espoused by his own teacher Shilabhadra, which derived from the Indian philosopher Dharmapala. Thus, although Hsüan-tsang is noted for having worked to disseminate a knowledge of the Consciousness-only doctrines, he taught only the version of those doctrines that derives from Dharmapala's *Treatise on the Establishment of the Consciousness-only System* and neglected other versions such as that expounded in Asanga's *Mahayana Samgraha.*

Without going into the details of this extremely complex matter, the version approved by Hsüan-tsang described eight types of consciousness, the most profound or deepest type being the *alaya* consciousness. In the teachings based upon the *Mahayana Samgraha,* however, a ninth type of consciousness is propounded, the *amala* consciousness, suggesting that this is the more highly developed version of the doctrine.

In other ways, too, the teachings that derive from Hsüan-tsang are a doctrinal regression. The Chinese Fa-hsiang and the Japanese Hosso sects, which revere Hsüan-tsang as their founder, for example, teach that all sentient beings may be classified into five categories, and that one category, the *icchantika,* or persons of incorrigible disbelief, are forever incapable of attaining enlightenment. This represents a retrogression from the teachings of the *Lotus Sutra* and the other Mahayana works that promise salvation to all beings, including the *icchantika.* Moreover, the Hosso Sect teaches that the One Vehicle expounded in the *Lotus Sutra* is merely an expedient teaching, and that the Three Vehicles, which the One Vehicle is designed to replace, is in fact the true teaching. Once again, this view represents a devolution from the *Lotus Sutra* teachings.

In the general development of Chinese Buddhism, therefore, Hsüan-tsang's teachings constitute a reversal of direction. Even before the appearance of T'ien-t'ai Chih-i, the schools of southern Buddhism in China had generally agreed that the *icchantika* are capable of attaining Buddhahood and that the Three Vehicles represent a kind of expedient teaching that is to be replaced by the One Vehicle doctrine. After the appearance of Chih-i, these views became even **more** widely accepted in Chinese Buddhist circles.

As a separate sect, the Fa-hsiang Sect was founded by K'uei-chi (632–82), Hsüan-tsang's principal disciple, who is also known as the Great Teacher Tz'u-en. He wrote a work on the *Lotus Sutra* entitled *Fa-hua Hsüan-tsan* in which he consciously addressed himself to the views regarding the *Lotus Sutra* put forth by Chih-i and, as we have seen, advanced contradictory views of his own. Instead of preaching universal salvation for all beings, he maintained that there are certain types of persons who can never hope to gain enlightenment.

In addition to the Fa-hsiang Sect, there is a second sect which derives from the teachings of Hsüan-tsang, namely the Chü-she (Japanese, Kusha) School, which takes its name from the fact that it is based upon the *Abhidharmakosha*, a work by the Indian philosopher Vasubandhu known in Chinese as the *Chü-she Lun* and in Japanese as the *Kusha Ron*. As I have explained in my earlier volume on Indian Buddhism, this work was written when Vasubandhu was a young man and was still an adherent of the Sarvastivada sect of the Hinayana. It presents a critical assessment of the doctrines of the sect as they pertain to the Abhidharma treatises, and thus serves as a convenient introduction to the basic ideas of Indian Buddhism. In Chinese and Japanese Buddhism it has been used as a kind of textbook for the training of persons who are entering the Buddhist clergy. The work was translated into Chinese by Paramartha and later retranslated by Hsüan-tsang; many of the latter's disciples and followers wrote commentaries on his translation of the work.

Useful as the work may be as an introduction to Buddhist philosophy it can hardly be regarded as a proper foundation for a separate sect of Buddhism. For one thing, it is a philosophical treatise, and hence not in the same class as the sutras, which are expositions of eternal and unchanging truths as set forth by the Buddha in the course of his preaching. In my view at least, a sect of Buddhism should found itself upon the teachings of the sutras, taking a particular sutra such as the *Lotus Sutra*, the *Nirvana Sutra*, or the *Flower Garland Sutra* and making the doctrines of that sutra the center of its teachings. But to found a sect upon a philosophical treatise written by an Indian philosopher who lived long after the time of the Buddha seems to be highly questionable.

However that may be, we cannot help noting that both of the sects that derive from Hsüan-tsang's teachings and translation activities, the Fa-hsiang Sect and the Chü-she Sect, tended to be highly abstract and philosophical in nature, and neither of them lasted for very long or had any great influence on the development of Chinese or Japanese Buddhism. It would seem that their teachings were too far removed from the realities of everyday life.

In his youth, Hsüan-tsang seems to have been fired with an ardent idealism, a determination to seek the truth that led him to embark on his long and difficult trip to India. One cannot help but admire his spirit of devotion and applaud him for carrying his pilgrimage to a successful conclusion. But, perhaps because of weariness brought on by his years of travel, his activities after his return to China seem disappointingly small in scale. Instead of working to disseminate the teachings to as wide an audience as possible, as a true man of religion would have done, he was content to spend his remaining years in the task of translation. True, translation is a step in the direction of propagation of the faith, and Hsüan-tsang certainly won great honor from Emperor T'ai-tsung and the members of his court for his religious endeavors and attracted many disciples who assisted him in his translation work. And yet the works that he chose to translate and the teachings he stressed were of a highly philosophical and abstruse nature, suitable perhaps for the study of scholars and members of the aristocracy, but lacking in the true Mahayana spirit, with its concern for the salvation of all humankind.

Partly this may be a reflection of the fact that the Buddhism that Hsüan-tsang found when he arrived in India was already in a marked state of decline. Of course he had no way of knowing this when he first set off on his journey. He believed that in going to the homeland of the Buddhist religion he would be able to gain the most thorough and accurate understanding of its teachings that it was possible to acquire. But in fact by Hsüan-tsang's time Chinese Buddhism was in a far more flourishing and creative stage than was the Buddhism of India. Around the fourth century, when philosophers such as Asanga and Vasubandhu dominated the world of Indian Buddhism, such was not the case. But afterward Buddhism in India declined steadily in vigor and influence. Meanwhile, Chinese Buddhism, having overcome the difficulties of the initial phases, advanced rapidly. With the development of the schools of southern Buddhism in the fifth and sixth centuries, and particularly with the appearance of such figures as Nan-yüeh Hui-ssu and T'ien-t'ai Chih-i, it may be said to have surpassed its Indian counterpart in importance. One feels that if Hsüan-tsang had taken more careful notice of the writings of these men, he might have been able to avoid the abstruseness and sterility which too often characterized his own teachings and those of his followers.

9. T'ang Buddhism and
the Achievement of Miao-lo Chan-jan

BUDDHISM IN THE REIGN OF EMPEROR HSÜAN-TSUNG

I would like in this chapter to discuss the life and accomplishment of Chan-jan (711–82), the sixth patriarch of T'ien-t'ai Buddhism if one counts Chih-i as the founder of the sect, the ninth patriarch if one counts Nagarjuna as the founder. He is often referred to as Ching-hsi Chan-jan because Ching-hsi was his birthplace, and he is also known by the posthumous title the Great Teacher Miao-lo, which derives from the fact that he lived at a temple in Lan-ling called the Miao-lo-ssu. He is credited with reviving the fortunes of the T'ien-t'ai Sect, which had fallen into decline after the death of Chih-i in 597.

Before proceeding to an examination of Chan-jan's life, however, I would like to look briefly at the political situation that prevailed at the time and the condition of Chinese Buddhism in general.

Chan-jan was born in 711, the year before the famous ruler Emperor Hsüan-tsung (685–762) came to the throne. The sixth sovereign of the T'ang dynasty, he did much to strengthen the position of the dynasty, and in fact the early years of his long reign are regarded as a period of model government. Chan-jan was born ten years after Li Po (701–62), one of China's most famous poets, and one year before Tu Fu (712–70), another of the great T'ang poets. His lifetime in fact corresponded with one of the most glorious eras in Chinese culture and literature, when the populous and flourishing T'ang capital city, Ch'ang-an, served as a crossroads of cultural exchange for all of eastern Asia.

The later years of Emperor Hsüan-tsung's reign, however, were marred by rebellion and chaos. The emperor, becoming increasingly infatuated with his beautiful concubine Yang Kuei-fei, neglected affairs of state to a dangerous degree. In 755, a military adventurer named An Lu-shan headed a revolt that in time obliged the emperor to flee from the capital to western China and relinquish the throne to his son. Forced by his soliders to order the execution of his beloved Yang Kuei-fei, he spent his closing years in sorrow and remorse.

The romance of Emperor Hsüan-tsung and Yang Kuei-fei and the events of the An Lu-shan rebellion are well known to Chinese and Japanese readers through the poetry of Li Po and Tu Fu, and in particular through the famous poem entitled *Song of Everlasting Regret* by Po Chü-i (772–846). By contrast, the career of Chan-jan, who lived at the same time as these events and worked to revive interest in the teachings of the T'ien-t'ai Sect, is relatively unknown, in spite of the great influence which Buddhism exerted upon the development of T'ang culture as a whole.

According to the *Record of the Lineage of the Buddha and the Patriarchs,* Chan-jan received imperial summonses from three T'ang rulers, Emperor Hsüan-tsung, Emperor Su-tsung (711–62) and Emperor Tai-tsung (726–79). On all three occasions, however, Chan-jan, who at this time was residing at Mount T'ien-t'ai, declined to respond to their invitations, giving sickness as his excuse. The question of just what his real reason was requires further study of the relations between the various Buddhist sects of the time and the T'ang imperial house. Scholars have suggested the following possibilities.

The T'ang dynasty was founded in 618 by Li Yüan when he overthrew the preceding Sui dynasty, though the real work of establishing the new dynasty was carried out by his son and successor, Li Shih-min, who is commonly known by his posthumous title T'ang T'ai-tsung. The Li family, of which the T'ang rulers were members, traced its ancestry back to Lao Tzu, the ancient philosopher and reputed founder of the Taoist religion. In 650, when the third T'ang ruler, Emperor Kao-tsung, came to the throne, he declared Taoism the official creed of the state. Thereafter, though Taoism and Buddhism often found themselves in a situation of confrontation during the years of the T'ang dynasty, the Taoist religion was on the whole given support and preferential treatment by the T'ang court, with Buddhism accorded a secondary position.

After Emperor Hsüan-tsung came to the throne in 712, he declared himself a believer in Taoism and set about taking measures to favor the Taoist religion, at the same time repressing Buddhism and ordering some thirty thousand Buddhist monks and nuns to return to lay life. Among the population as a whole, however, Buddhism continued to enjoy great popularity, if anything gaining in power and influence. Emperor Hsüan-tsung therefore apparently felt the time was not right to move more openly against Buddhism. Instead, in the twenty-sixth year of the K'ai-yüan era, 738 by the Western calendar, the emperor set about establishing officially sponsored Buddhist temples in all the prefectures of China, which went by the name of K'ai-yüan temples.

Parenthetically, it may be noted that three years later, in 741, the Japanese ruler Emperor Shomu (r. 724–49) set up a similar system of state-sponsored temples in the various provinces of Japan, the *kokubunji*. Japan was at this time in close contact with China, sending embassies to the Chinese court at frequent intervals, and it is probable that Emperor Shomu's move to establish official temples throughout the country was modeled after that of Emperor Hsüan-tsung.

It has been suggested that Emperor Hsüan-tsung's objective in setting up this network of government temples was to gain tighter control over the Buddhist community. In other words, having realized that outright suppression of the Buddhist religion in favor of its Taoist rival would not be practical because of the wide popular support that Buddhism enjoyed, he decided to adopt a conciliatory policy and to acquire greater influence over the activities of the Buddhist community and its followers through the establishment of officially sponsored temples.

Scholars have speculated that the reason Chan-jan did not respond to the invitation from Emperor Hsüan-tsung was that he had already surmised where the emperor's true intentions lay. The invitation from Emperor Hsüan-tsung came toward the end of the T'ien-pao era, which lasted from 742 to 755—in other words, in the closing years of the emperor's reign. Its ostensible purpose was to congratulate Chan-jan on the completion of the first draft of his great commentary on Chih-i's *Great Concentration and Insight, Mo-ho Chih-kuan Fu-hsing-chuan Hung-chüeh.* But Chan-jan, far from being moved to gratitude by the honor, summarily declined the emperor's invitation to come to the capital, an indication of how he felt about the prospect of such a move.

Another reason why Chan-jan did not respond to the imperial invitation was probably the fact that Emperor Hsüan-tsung was at this time showing special favor to the Chen-yen Sect of Buddhism, the doctrines commonly referred to as Tantric or Esoteric Buddhism. As pointed out by Nichiren Daishonin in his second letter to Ueno-dono (*Ueno-dono Gohenji* No. 2 or *Tsuchi Mochi Kuyō Gosho*), it was during the reign of Emperor Hsüan-tsung that Esoteric Buddhism was first introduced to China.

The Indian monk Shubhakarasimha (637–735), who is regarded as the founder of Chen-yen Buddhism in China, came to Ch'ang-an in 716, the fifth year of Emperor Hsüan-tsung's reign. The emperor, who had a predilection for anything novel, welcomed the Indian monk, set him up in quarters within the inner palace, and encouraged him to carry out the practices of the sect and to engage in making Chinese translations of its principal texts such as the *Mahavairochana Sutra.*

Four years later, in 720, two other Indian monks of the Esoteric Sect, Vajrabodhi (671–741) and Amoghavajra (705–74), came to Ch'ang-an and were likewise treated with great favor by Emperor Hsüan-tsung.

These three monks, Shubhakarasimha, Vajrabodhi, and Amoghavajra, came to be referred to as the Three Bodhisattvas of the K'ai-yüan Era, and they numbered among their supporters not only Emperor Hsüan-tsung himself but many of his most influential officials and military leaders, as well as numerous persons of less exalted station.

As pointed out by scholars of Buddhism, one of the reasons for this ready acceptance of the Esoteric teachings was the fact that Esoteric Buddhism places great emphasis upon incantations and other magical or semimagical rituals. This type of magical element had not generally been known in earlier Buddhism, but it was an important part of the Taoist religion, and as we have seen, the T'ang court paid special honor to Taoism. The monk Amoghavajra was particularly noted for his magic formulas, rain-making ceremonies, and other incantatory practices. From the time of his arrival in Ch'ang-an in 720 until his death in 774 at the age of seventy, he enjoyed great esteem with three rulers in succession, emperors Hsüan-tsung, Su-tsung, and Tai-tsung, and dominated Buddhist circles in the capital.

These three rulers, as we have seen, are the ones who sent imperial invitations to Chan-jan. Chan-jan's refusal to accept any of these invitations is no doubt an indication that he did not wish to become associated with a court that lent its support so wholeheartedly to the Esoteric teachings. The power and authority exercised by the T'ang ruler at this time was virtually absolute, at least within the sphere of Chinese influence, and it must have required great courage on Chan-jan's part to decline the invitations extended to him by the three emperors. At the same time, he must have had very compelling reasons for doing so.

Ill health was the reason he gave for his refusals to accept the imperial summons, though this would seem to be no more than an excuse, since in the reign of Emperor Su-tsung he traveled as far as Nan-yüeh in southern China, and in the reign of Emperor Tai-tsung made a pilgrimage to Mount Wu-t'ai in the far north. His basic reason for declining to accept the imperial invitation to journey to the capital was no doubt the fact that he saw no real advantage in doing so, since it might place him in a position where he would have to compromise the principles of the T'ien-t'ai doctrine. To Chan-jan, these principles constituted the orthodox teaching of the Buddhist religion, and he had no desire to see them sullied by the heresies of the other sects.

DOCTRINAL PROFUNDITY AND THE PROBLEM
OF PROPAGATION

Before the appearance of Chan-jan on the scene, the T'ien-t'ai Sect underwent what has been termed its first period of eclipse. When Chih-i died in 597, Chang-an Kuan-ting was chosen from among his three thousand or more disciples to act as his successor. Chang-an in time was succeeded by Chih-wei (d. 680), Hui-wei (634–713) and Hsüan-lang (673–754) in turn. But during the hundred or more years after the passing of Chang-an Kuan-ting, the T'ien-t'ai Sect failed to prosper. If we examine the reasons for that failure, we can better appreciate the importance of the role which Chan-jan was later to play.

First, as I have already mentioned in my discussion of Chih-i in chapter 7, the teachings of the T'ien-t'ai Sect were in a sense too profound and complex or too elevated in philosophical nature to be comprehensible to ordinary lay believers. This fact naturally made it difficult to propagate the T'ien-t'ai teachings on a wide scale and hindered the growth of the sect. It would appear that Chih-i himself was aware of this shortcoming in his doctrines.

Though Chih-i's disciples numbered over three thousand, it is said that the only one who truly understood the teachings of the master as they took shape in his three major works was Chang-an Kuan-ting, his successor. And, as we have seen, though Chang-an recorded Chih-i's lectures on the *Lotus Sutra* and compiled them into *Words and Phrases of the Lotus Sutra,* it took him forty-two years of labor before he was able to put the material into finished form. This fact alone suggests that the teachings of the T'ien-t'ai Sect were of a depth and complexity that rendered them very difficult to comprehend by ordinary members of the Buddhist community in

China at that time. At best, probably no more than a few key phrases or slogans were understood by the followers of the T'ien-t'ai or the other Buddhist sects of the period.

It is interesting to note in this connection how one such phrase was borrowed and incorporated into the teachings of another sect. The Indian monk Shubhakarasimha had a Chinese disciple named I-hsing (683–727). In an earlier period in his life, I-hsing had studied the teachings of the T'ien-t'ai Sect, but in 721 he was ordered by Emperor Hsüan-tsung to take up residence in the imperial palace and to assist Shubhakarasimha in making a Chinese translation of the *Mahavairochana Sutra*. In addition, he compiled a commentary on the sutra, *Annotations on the Mahavairochana Sutra,* which, along with the translation, was used in propagating the teachings of Esoteric Buddhism.

As we have seen, Esoteric Buddhism as it was first imported from India was concerned mainly with incantations and magic formulas and had very little in the way of philosophical content. But I-hsing, in compiling his commentary on the *Mahavairochana Sutra,* appears to have borrowed the concept of "the true entity of all phenomena," which is associated with Chinese Buddhism and the teachings of the T'ien-t'ai Sect in particular, and claimed to have discovered this concept in the doctrines of Esoteric Buddhism as they are set forth in the *Mahavairochana Sutra.* Thus the T'ien-t'ai teachings were employed to enrich the philosophical content of Esoteric Buddhism, though without acknowledgment of the fact.

But to return to the question of why the T'ien-t'ai Sect failed to thrive in the years following Chang-an's death, some scholars suggest that part of the difficulty may have been the fact that the sect had its headquarters at Mount T'ien-t'ai south of the Yangtze, which was far removed from the T'ang capital. By contrast, the other important sects of the time such as the Chen-yen Sect, the Fa-hsiang Sect founded by Hsüan-tsang and Tz'u-en, the Lü (Vinaya) sect of Nan-shan Tao-hsüan and I-ching, and the Hua-yen Sect of Fa-tsang all had their bases of activity in or around Ch'ang-an and hence flourished in the capital area.

Though there may be some truth in this assertion, we should at

the same time consider the possibility that this geographical isola-
tion from the capital area on the part of the T'ien-t'ai Sect was
perhaps required in order to insure the purity of its teachings and
protect it from involvement in political issues. It may therefore
not necessarily have been a disadvantage.

But let us turn now to what is known of Chan-jan's life. He was
born in a place called Ching-hsi in Kiangsu, and hence is sometimes referred to as the Sage of Ching-hsi. His father was a Confucian scholar and he himself was trained in the teachings of Confucianism. Had his life followed the ordinary pattern, he would
have taken the civil service examination and, when he had passed
it successfully, would have embarked on a career as a government
official. But at the age of seventeen—sixteen by Western reckoning—he traveled to eastern Chekiang to continue his studies,
and there met a monk named Fang-yen of Chin-hua who instructed
him in the fundamentals of the T'ien-t'ai doctrine. As a result of
this encounter, he determined to abandon the pursuit of a worldly
career and instead to devote himself to the study of the principles
of the Buddhist teaching.

Little is known of the identity of Fang-yen. Some accounts say
that he was a disciple of Hsüan-lang, the fifth successor in the line
of Chih-i's teachings, who has already been mentioned above;
others say that he was a disciple of Hsüan-lang's predecessor Hui-
wei, and hence a fellow student of Hsüan-lang.

In 730, when Chan-jan was twenty by Chinese reckoning, he
journeyed to Hsüan-lang's residence on Mount Tso-hsi and applied directly to him for instruction in the T'ien-t'ai teachings.
According to the account of the meeting in the *Lineage of the Buddha and the Patriarchs,* Hsüan-lang instantly recognized that the
young man before him had the potential to become an outstanding
leader in the interpretation and propagation of the Way.

For certain reasons, Chan-jan did not don clerical robes and
officially enter the Buddhist priesthood until the age of thirty-
eight. But in the meantime, while he was still garbed as a Confucian
scholar, Hsüan-lang set about teaching Chan-jan all that he knew
about the philosophical doctrines and meditation practices of the

T'ien-t'ai Sect, an indication of the faith he had in the young man's future. Hsüan-lang was by this time reaching the close of his eighty-two-year life span and no doubt had been waiting hopefully for the appearance of a disciple with just such ability and promise as Chan-jan displayed.

In the T'ang capital cities of Ch'ang-an and Lo-yang at this time, various schools of Buddhism flourished, including Esoteric Buddhism, the Consciousness-only Sect, the Hua-yen Sect, and the Ch'an Sect. By contrast, the profound truths of the T'ien-t'ai Sect, which represented the most orthodox version of the Buddha's teachings in China, barely managed to maintain an existence in the far-off mountains of the T'ien-t'ai range in Chekiang. Hsüan-lang no doubt yearned to see the T'ien-t'ai teachings propagated as rapidly as possible throughout the four corners of the great T'ang empire.

Chan-jan was undoubtedly acutely aware of his teacher's wishes and the trust that the latter placed in him. Hsüan-lang died in 754, when Chan-jan was forty-three years of age, and Chan-jan thereupon became his heir and successor in the T'ien-t'ai line. In the years that followed, he set about traveling throughout the country and preaching the T'ien-t'ai doctrines, and for the first time the sect became widely known in China.

Chan-jan's Achievements and Their Importance

Let us turn now to Chan-jan's thought and writings. His writings fall into two main categories, exegetical works and polemical writings. Among the former, the most important are his commentaries on Chih-i's three major works. These are *Fa-hua Hsüan-i Shih-ch'ien* in ten volumes, a commentary on Chih-i's *Profound Meaning of the Lotus Sutra; Fa-hua Wen-chü Chi* in ten chapters, a commentary on the *Words and Phrases of the Lotus Sutra;* and *Mo-ho Chih-kuan Fu-hsing-chuan Hung-chüeh* in ten chapters, a commentary on *Great Concentration and Insight.* Several other works such as *The General Meaning of Great Concentration and Insight* and *Essentials of the*

Commentary on Great Concentration and Insight likewise deal with Chih-i's teachings, and he also produced a condensation of Chih-i's commentary on the *Vimalakirti Sutra* entitled *Wei-mo Ching Lüeh-shu.*

The polemical writings are on the whole designed to refute the teachings of the Hua-yen, Fa-hsiang, and Ch'an sects. Particularly noteworthy are the *Chin-p'i Lun* in one volume, also known as the *Chin-kang-p'i Lun,* a refutation of Hua-yen doctrines; the *Fa-hua Wu-pai-wen Lun* in three volumes, a refutation of the Fa-hsiang teachings on the *Lotus Sutra;* and the *Chih-kuan I-li* in two volumes, which criticizes the meditation practices of the Ch'an sect.

Since Nichiren Daishonin in his writings so often quotes Chan-jan's commentaries on Chih-i's three major works, these commentaries are quite familiar to those of us who are followers of the Daishonin's Buddhism. The Daishonin's customary practice, as shown in the *Record of the Orally Transmitted Teachings,* his lectures on the *Lotus Sutra,* was to first quote a passage from one of the major writings of T'ien-t'ai Chih-i, and then quote Chan-jan's commentary on the passage, in this way bringing out the full meaning of the passage and the doctrine expounded in it.

The second group of Chan-jan's writings, the polemical works, give a good picture of how the T'ien-t'ai teachings compare to those of the other sects of the time. By the middle years of the T'ang dynasty, when Chan-jan was active, the doctrines of the various sects of Chinese Buddhism had more or less reached their definitive form. Chan-jan studied each of these doctrines in turn and then set about making clear how the teachings of the T'ien-t'ai Sect differed from each. The polemical writings that resulted demonstrate Chan-jan's concern for the refutation of error and his eagerness to convert others to the teachings of his own sect, in other words, his *shakubuku* spirit.

In spite of the interest which these polemical writings hold, there is little doubt that Chan-jan's real accomplishment rests with his exegetical works, particularly the accurate and detailed commentaries on Chih-i's three major writings. It is in fact difficult to imagine how Chih-i's writings would have fared in the world if they had not had the commentaries of Chan-jan appended to them.

Some indication of what their fate might have been, however, is provided by the fact that, although the Chinese monk Chien-chen (688–763), who came to Japan in 753, brought with him copies of Chih-i's three major writings, they had not yet at that time been provided with Chan-jan's commentaries and hence proved to be so difficult to comprehend that they had virtually no influence in Japan. It was only later, when the Japanese monk Saicho (767–822) journeyed to China and studied the writings of Chih-i and the commentaries of Chan-jan under two of Chan-jan's disciples, Tao-sui and Hsing-man, that the doctrines of the T'ien-t'ai Sect were fully and correctly understood by a Japanese and transmitted to Japan, where they formed the basis of the Tendai Sect.

We may safely say that Chan-jan's commentaries on the three major writings of Chih-i constitute his greatest achievement, a work that he labored at throughout most of his life. He spared no amount of time and effort in ferreting out the meaning of Chih-i's writings, and in the end was able to make himself a thorough master of the T'ien-t'ai doctrines, which represented the loftiest and most complex philosophical system of all Chinese Buddhism at that time. Specialists in the field all agree that, when attempting to fathom the meaning in Chih-i's difficult writings, one can do no better than to rely upon the guidance of Chan-jan's masterful commentaries.

It should also be noted that, while Chan-jan set about elucidating the doctrines expounded by Chih-i through his commentaries on Chih-i's writings, he also in some ways expanded those doctrines and deepened the philosophical tenets of the sect. Outstanding examples of this latter activity are found in the doctrine of the ten onenesses set forth in the *Fa-hua Hsüan-i Shih-ch'ien* and the doctrine of the eternal truth and its manifestations under changing circumstances set forth in *The General Meaning* and the *Chin-p'i Lun*.

In *The Profound Meaning of the Lotus Sutra,* Chih-i had expounded the ten mystic principles of the theoretical teaching of the *Lotus Sutra* and the ten mystic principles of the essential teaching of the *Lotus*. Chan-jan in his *Fa-hua Hsüan-i Shih-ch'ien* comments on this passage and explains that the ten mystic principles of both the theoretical and the essential teachings are included in the ten onenesses. The ten onenesses are (1) the oneness of body and mind; (2) the oneness of the internal and the external; (3) the oneness of the goal of practice and the true nature of phenomena; (4) the oneness of cause and effect; (5) the oneness of the impure and the pure; (6) the oneness of life and its environment; (7) the oneness of self and others; (8) the oneness of thought, word, and deed; (9) the oneness of the theoretical and the essential teachings; and (10) the oneness of benefit. I will not attempt here to explain the full meaning of each of these ten categories or principles. We may simply note that the point of Chan-jan's doctrine is that terms which appear to be opposites, such as body and mind or pure and impure, can be viewed as a single entity. Thus, for example, considered from a general point of view, body and mind constitute a single concept, though when they are considered from a specific point of view they can be broken down into the two categories of body and mind.

Chan-jan probably felt that Chih-i, in simply listing the names of the ten mystic principles of the theoretical and the essential teachings, had not explained the matter clearly enough to be fully comprehensible to readers. He therefore added his own explanations, giving the mystic principles a more dynamic interpretation. In his doctrine of the ten onenesses, therefore, he was adding a new concept to the T'ien-t'ai philosophy. Here we see him not simply commenting on and explicating Chih-i's teachings, but laboring to expand them and give them greater philosophical depth.

In *The General Meaning,* Chan-jan for the first time enunciates the doctrine of the eternal truth and its manifestations under changing circumstances (*chen-ju sui-yüan*). According to this doctrine, the absolute mind embraces all the phenomena of the universe, and hence it has within it both the aspects of eternal truth and of constant changeability. The two conditions of being eternally unchanging and at the same changeable in accordance with the varying circumstances constitute a single entity, and because the mind of the individual contains these two aspects, it can embrace all the varying phenomena of the universe.

This doctrine would appear to be Chan-jan's answer to certain objections that had been brought against the T'ien-t'ai teachings by philosophers of the Hua-yen Sect. Chih-i in his *Great Concentration and Insight* had stated that "mind is identical with the manifold phenomena; the manifold phenomena are identical with mind." But the objection was made that such a laconic statement failed to explain how the countless phenomena of the universe are produced or come forth from the mind.

The explanation of the process by which phenomena, through the action of causation, are produced from the *tathata,* the absolute mind or eternal truth, had originally been expounded in *The Awakening of Faith in the Mahayana,* a text attributed to the Indian poet and philosopher Ashvaghosha. The scholars of the Hua-yen Sect borrowed this explanation and used it in their own philosophy. On that basis, they then set about criticizing the theory of three thousand worlds in a single instant of thought set forth by Chih-i because it fails to explain how the three thousand worlds of phenomena can be created or be present in a single life-moment, i.e., it does not clarify the relationship between the absolute and the phenomenal. Chan-jan in his *General Meaning* and *Chin-p'i Lun* undertook to reply to these criticisms.

The *Chin-p'i Lun* is Chan-jan's last work, and in it the doctrine of the eternal truth and its manifestations in changing circumstances is enunciated most clearly. Thus he states: "The ten thousand phenomena are the same as the eternal truth because they partake of the nature of unchangeability. The eternal truth is the same as the ten thousand phenomena because it partakes of the nature of changeability." In other words, the eternal truth or the absolute should be perceived as a single entity that embraces both the aspects of changeability and unchangeability. The expounders of the Hua-yen philosophy had tended to emphasize simply the changeable aspects or the process by which the absolute becomes manifest in the phenomenal, whereas the T'ien-t'ai doctrine places equal emphasis upon both aspects and hence represents a profounder and more comprehensive view.

The *Chin-p'i Lun* is also important because in it Chan-jan expounds the doctrine that inanimate and insentient things such as plants or stones are endowed with the Buddha nature. As he states, "A plant, a tree, a pebble, a speck of dust—each has the innate Buddha nature, along with the other causes and conditions needed to attain Buddhahood." In this doctrine, Chan-jan refutes the argument put forward by Ch'eng-kuan, the fourth patriarch of the Hua-yen Sect, who asserted that insentient beings do not have the Buddha nature. Chan-jan's doctrine derives naturally from the views we have described above concerning the identity of the absolute and the phenomenal and represents an important addition to the T'ien-t'ai philosophy.

Before Chan-jan's time, the Hua-yen doctrines were looked upon as the highest and most logically advanced expression of Buddhist philosophy, but Chan-jan reversed that situation and succeeded in placing the T'ien-t'ai teachings in the foremost position, expanding them and bringing them to their most highly developed form.

Chan-jan also played an important role in the process by which the T'ien-t'ai doctrines were transmitted to Japan. As we have already seen, when the Japanese monk Saicho came to China in search of a fuller understanding of the T'ien-ta'i doctrines, he studied under two of Chan-jan's disciples, Tao-sui and Hsing-man. Through their instruction and the writings of Chan-jan, he was able to gain an accurate and thorough understanding of the T'ien-t'ai teachings and to propagate them in Japan after his return.

In addition to Tao-sui and Hsing-man, Chan-jan had other important disciples such as Ming-k'uang, author of the *P'u-sa Chieh-shu,* and Chih-yün, author of the *Wen-chü Ssu-chih Chi,* both names that are well known in Japanese Buddhist circles even today. After Chan-jan's time, the T'ien-t'ai Sect, along with Chinese Buddhism as a whole, fell into a decline, entering what has been called its second period of eclipse. But, thanks to the efforts of Chan-jan and his disciples and the Japanese monk Saicho, the teachings of the sect were successfully transmitted to Japan and flourished there long after they had all but disappeared in China.

Liang-su, another of Chan-jan's disciples, in the grave inscription that he wrote for Chan-jan after the latter's death, described him as the "restorer of the T'ien-t'ai Sect," and historians of Chinese Buddhism have concurred in that judgment. After the eclipse which it had suffered following Chih-i's death, the sect was restored to prominence largely through the efforts of Chan-jan. Unlike so many Buddhist leaders of the time such as K'uei-chi of the Fa-hsiang Sect, Fa-tsang of the Hua-yen Sect, or the Indian exponents of Esoteric Buddhism, Shubhakarasimha and Amoghavajra, who associated themselves closely with the T'ang court and capital, Chan-jan remained aloof from secular circles and concerns, devoting himself to the search for philosophical understanding and the training of his disciples, in order, as the *Lotus Sutra* puts it, "to insure the perpetuation of the Law."

In one sense his life may seem to have been a quiet one, devoted as it was to study, writing, and the training of disciples. But he was anything but passive in his defense of what he regarded as the true principles of Buddhism. He set out vigorously to refute the errors of others, traveling widely in both northern and southern China, and up the Yangtze River far to the west, combating error and spreading the doctrines of the T'ien-t'ai Sect. As the restorer of the sect's fortunes, he was thoroughly a man of action, devoting himself unsparingly to the pursuit of his ideals.

10. The Buddhist Persecutions

In the preceding chapters we have traced the history of Buddhism in China over a period of some seven or eight hundred years, from the time of its introduction to China around the beginning of the Christian era to the revival of the T'ien-t'ai doctrines under the leadership of Chan-jan, the Great Teacher Miao-lo, in the eighth century, paying particular attention to those groups in Chinese Buddhism that revere the *Lotus Sutra*. In this closing chapter, I would like to approach the subject from a somewhat different point of view, describing the trials and persecutions that the Buddhist faith was at times subjected to in China and examining the relations that existed between Buddhism and the native Chinese religions and systems of belief such as Confucianism and Taoism, and between Buddhism and the state.

The Chinese customarily refer to the major Buddhist persecutions as the "Three Wu and One Tsung," because three of them took place during the reign of emperors whose posthumous name contained the word *wu* and the fourth occurred during the reign of an emperor whose posthumous name is Shih-tsung, hence the "One Tsung." Exhaustive studies of these great persecutions have been carried out by the eminent Japanese Buddhologist Zenryu Tsukamoto, and these will be utilized as the basis of our discussion here.

153

We will begin with the "Three Wu," the persecutions carried out under Emperor T'ai-wu of the Northern Wei, Emperor Wu of the Northern Chou, and Emperor Wu-tsung of the T'ang. The Buddhist community in China was subjected, however, to far more persecutions and harassments then those represented by the "Three Wu and One Tsung" alone. These constitute merely the most notable persecutions, those carried out with the greatest thoroughness and under overall government supervision.

First of all it is important to consider the fact that the emperors who conducted the first three persecutions all bear posthumous names with the element *wu* in them. When a ruler died in China, it was customary to select a posthumous name for him that in some way reflected his character or the nature of his reign. The word *wu* means warlike or militaristic and was assigned to rulers whose reigns placed particular emphasis upon conquests or the exercise of military might.

Rulers everywhere in the world, Chinese emperors included, tend to place great stress upon national traditions and ways of thought when they wish to embark on military ventures, at the same time displaying hostility toward foreign creeds and ways of thought. In this way they seek to create a sense of national consciousness among their subjects and to rouse their patriotic ardor so that they can more easily be led into war against foreign opponents. This is precisely what happened in the case of the "Three Wu" persecutions in China, each of them taking place at a time when the ruler was engaged in military operations.

The first of these persecutions occurred in the reign of Emperor T'ai-wu of the Northern Wei. The Northern Wei dynasty, which lasted from 386 to 534, was founded by the T'o-pa group of the Hsien-pei, a nomadic people living north of China who invaded China and established a dynasty ruling over the northern part of the country. Emperor T'ai-wu, the third ruler of the dynasty, devoted himself to attacks on the Shensi and Kansu regions in a drive to extend the area under his control.

Emperor T'ai-wu came to the throne in 424, and in the following year began his attacks on the Shensi area, expanding the control of the Northern Wei in a westerly direction. In this same year (425) he established a Taoist temple known as the T'ien-shih-tao-t'an in the Wei capital. In 429, Emperor T'ai-wu launched attacks on the Juan-juan, a nomadic people of Mongolia who frequently invaded the borders of the Wei, and in 439 he began attacks on the Kansu region to the west. Thus the years of his reign, which lasted until 452, were largely devoted to militaristic expansion, his aim no doubt being to bring the entire area of northern China under his control.

In 431, while these military activities were in progress, he ordered that a Taoist temple be set up in each of the districts in the area under his rule. A hundred persons were assigned to each temple for the exercise of religious duties. With this move, the emperor in effect made Taoism the official religion of the state. Shortly after, he began taking steps to suppress the Buddhist religion, Taoism's chief rival. In 438 he issued an edict ordering that all Buddhist monks under the age of fifty be returned to secular life. In the first month of 446, he led his troops to Ch'ang-an to put down a revolt that had broken out in the Shensi region, and in the third month of the same year officially ordered the abolishment of the Buddhist religion.

According to the edict issued at that time, any person found guilty of fashioning a Buddhist image would be put to death along with all the members of his family. At the same time, the local officials were ordered to burn and destroy all Buddhist temples, images and scriptures in the areas under their jurisdiction, and all Buddhist monks, regardless of age, were to be put to death.

Records of the period reveal that in fact local divisions of the army were dispatched to loot and burn the Buddhist temples, and all monks and nuns were forced to return to secular life. Any who attempted to flee or to go into hiding were pursued and taken captive and their heads cut off and displayed as a warning to the populace. The persecution was thus extremely severe and thorough-going. It is said that, as a result, not a single Buddhist temple or a single monk or nun was to be found in the entire land of the Northern Wei.

What factors could have led the government to embark on such a drastic suppression of Buddhism? First was the fact that the Buddhist monasteries were looked on as profitless and unproductive bodies in society and the members of the clergy as evaders of military conscription. The initial order to restore all monks under the age of fifty to secular life was no doubt intended to increase the number of men eligible for military service. In other words, from the point of view of the Chinese state, particularly in a period of wartime, the Buddhist clergy, intoning their sutras and preaching the doctrines of a foreign religion, were no more than privileged idlers who contributed nothing to society.

This fact becomes particularly apparent with the second of the "Three Wu" persecutions, that carried out by Emperor Wu of the Northern Chou, which ruled over northwestern China from 557 to 581. Emperor Wu came to the throne in 560 at the age of eighteen and immediately began making plans to attack the state of Northern Ch'i, which occupied the area of northeastern China. From the very first he thus committed himself to a militaristic policy, personally taking the lead in training troops, preparing armaments and laboring to heighten morale.

In 574, on the seventeenth day of the fifth month of the lunar calendar, Emperor Wu issued an edict banning both the Buddhist and Taoist religions. Accounts report that temples dating back several hundreds of years were leveled to the ground, Buddhist images were melted down, scriptures were burned, and some three million monks and nuns were returned to secular life, though the last figure may seem difficult to credit. In the seventh month of the following year, 575, Emperor Wu gathered his generals and military leaders about him and proclaimed the initiation of an attack on the Northern Ch'i. Before long, massive numbers of troops were pouring over the border into the neighboring state.

This persecution carried out by Emperor Wu of the Northern Chou is unusual in that it struck not only at Buddhism but at its rival, Taoism, as well. It is said that the bronze recovered by melting down Buddhist images was used to mint new currency, reminding one of how the Japanese government during the Pacific

War confiscated bells from Buddhist temples throughout the country and melted them down to use in the production of armaments. In order to insure victory in his campaign against the Northern Ch'i, Emperor Wu evidently felt that the entire population of the country should be organized in support of his armies, and this meant suppressing religious organizations and returning their members to lay life so that they might join in the war effort.

Emperor Wu's attack did in fact prove successful. He crushed the enemy in the closing months of 576, and in the first month of 577 the emperor himself entered the Northern Ch'i capital city of Yeh, where he decreed that the suppression of Buddhism be carried out in the newly conquered territory of the Northern Ch'i as well. As a result, the Buddhist persecution came to affect the entire area of northern China, and for a time all traces of the Buddhist religion disappeared from the region.

This persecution occurred just around the time when Chih-i was active in the area of southern China, and when Buddhism in northern China, particularly in the area under the control of the Northern Ch'i, was in a highly flourishing condition. It thus constituted a sudden and terrible reversal of fortune for the Buddhist religion in China.

The Background of the Buddhist Persecutions

Another fact that strikes us when we examine the history of the Buddhist persecutions in China is that in so many cases they came about as a result of conflicts or rivalry between Buddhism and the older traditional religions or systems of thought in China, particularly Confucianism and Taoism. In all cases, we find that there was some influential Taoist or Confucian adviser who was close to the ruler and who persuaded him to embark upon a course of anti-Buddhist activity.

Since this point also throws important light on the relationship between religion and the state in traditional Chinese society, let us examine the situation as it existed in the major Buddhist persecutions. Emperor T'ai-wu of the Northern Wei, as we have seen, was an enthusiastic supporter of Taoism and not only established an imposing Taoist temple in the capital but went on to order the establishment of government-sponsored Taoist temples in the various administrative districts throughout the country, thus making Taoism the official doctrine of the state.

Earlier, however, when Emperor T'ai-wu first came to the throne, he displayed a tolerant attitude toward Buddhism, and even took part in the celebrations held on the eighth day of the fourth lunar month in honor of the Buddha's birthday, when Buddhist images were paraded through the streets of the capital and the emperor paid homage to them by showering them with flowers. Buddhism at this time enjoyed great popularity throughout the area of northern China, and Emperor T'ai-wu, descended as he was from nomadic invaders, no doubt felt obliged in this way to give recognition to the faith of the masses under his rule.

Among the emperor's close associates, however, was one Ts'ui Hao, a Chinese scholar who had a great hatred for the Buddhist religion. Eventually he rose to high position in the government, and at the same time succeeded in promoting a Taoist practitioner named K'ou Ch'ien-chih to a post among the ruler's confidants. These two men then proceeded to win the emperor over to enthusiastic support of the Taoist teachings, and in time incited him to carry out measures to suppress Buddhism.

The Taoist K'ou Ch'ien-chih seems to have been a rather questionable individual who carried out his religious practices in a cave and, among various accomplishments, produced a Taoist work in sixty volumes that he claimed had been dictated to him by the heavenly deities. Ts'ui Hao likewise was of dubious character, and the emperor at first was inclined to be suspicious of his advice, but through eloquence and persistent offering of counsel, he in the end persuaded the emperor to trust his words.

History displays many examples of political leaders who, when they were at the height of their power, allowed themselves to be talked into employing men of uncertain character or bent, usually with disastrous results. Emperor T'ai-wu, an example of such a ruler, was persuaded to launch a persecution of Buddhism that for a period raged with great fury throughout the area under the rule of the Northern Wei. It was not long, however, before Ts'ui Hao's actions began to arouse widespread opposition, and in 450 he was executed along with all the members of his family. The Buddhist persecution did not officially come to an end until the death of Emperor T'ai-wu in 454, but in the closing years of his reign, when both K'ou Ch'ien-chih and Ts'ui Hao had disappeared from the scene, the measures against the religion were gradually relaxed.

In the case of the Buddhist persecution carried out under Emperor Wu of the Northern Chou dynasty, there were similar sinister figures in the background, the principal one being a man from Szechwan named Wei Yüan-sung.

The Northern Chou dynasty had been founded by members of the Yü-wen family, descendants of the nomadic people known as the Hsien-pei, and had its capital at Ch'ang-an. Because Ch'ang-an had been the site of the ancient Chou-dynasty capital, the Yü-wen rulers chose to call their dynasty Chou, and did their best to imitate the benevolent government of the ancient Chou sage-rulers, King Wen and King Wu, who are so often extolled in the Confucian classics, adopting Confucian teachings as the basis of their rule. When Emperor Wu came to the throne of the Northern Chou in 560, he invited Confucian scholars to be his advisers in government and observed Confucian rituals and principles in the ordering of the state.

In 567, when Emperor Wu was twenty-five, a Buddhist monk named Wei Yüan-sung, who was noted for his eccentric words and behavior, submitted a memorial to the throne in which he argued that the temples and monks heretofore known in China were not representative of the true Buddhist teachings. He therefore proposed that these traditional forms of Buddhism be done away with and that a new Buddhist church be organized that would embrace the entire nation and its population in a single great temple. To insure the attractiveness of his scheme, he proposed that the Chou ruler should head the new temple, representing a manifestation of the Tathagata, or Buddha, himself.

On the basis of Wei Yüan-sung's proposal, Emperor Wu did in fact ban both Buddhism and Taoism in 574. But he would probably not have carried out such an action if the Buddhist community itself had not been guilty of certain abuses. As a matter of fact, many of the temples had grown to awesome proportions and the ecclesiastical officials had acquired great wealth and power. The whole religious community had come to constitute a kind of self-governing body outside the control of the secular authorities. Moreover, many monks and nuns could not even read or recite the sacred texts in proper fashion, having only joined the religious order in hopes of insuring themselves a life of safety and ease.

To make matters worse, when Emperor Wu first came to the throne, he had assembled scholarly representatives of the Buddhist and Taoist religions and the Confucian teachings and set them debating, hoping in this way to promote harmony and cooperation among the three groups. But the Buddhists and Taoists had proceeded to attack each other with great acrimony, and the disgust inspired in the emperor by such behavior, it would seem, was one of the factors that in time led him to order the abolition of the two religions.

This disgust, however, and the abuses within the Buddhist community, would most likely not in themselves have been sufficient cause to trigger the kind of severe persecution that in time resulted. As a final factor, we must note the machinations of another figure, a Taoist priest named Chang Pin, who gained access to the emperor and who worked hand in hand with Wei Yüan-sung to stir up his antagonism against Buddhism. In the end, their efforts, along with the emperor's military preparations and his disillusionment with both the Buddhists and the Taoists, prompted him to issue his decree in 574 banning both religions.

The third of the "Three Wu" Buddhist persecutions, which took place under Emperor Wu-tsung of the T'ang, displayed many of the same characteristics as the persecutions we have discussed above, though the situation was somewhat more complicated and the scale of the persecution was far greater than anything previously encountered. It occurred when the dynasty, beset by wars and rebellions, was already drawing to a close, and it so thoroughly weakened Buddhism that the religion was never able to recover its former vigor.

Known also as the Hui-ch'ang Persecution because it took place during the Hui-ch'ang era, the movement began in 840, when Emperor Wu-tsung first ascended the throne, and proceeded by carefully planned steps, culminating in an edict in the eighth month of 845 that summed up the results of the persecution and revealed that the Buddhist religion was virtually being wiped out. The movement was noteworthy in that, unlike the previous persecutions, it affected all of China rather than the northern area alone. This meant that the great southern centers of Buddhism, which had heretofore escaped harassment, were all affected.

Emperor Wu-tsung had shown strong tendencies in favor of Taoism even before he came to the throne. As we have mentioned earlier, the T'ang imperial house belonged to the Li family, which traced its ancestry back to Lao Tzu, the founder of Taoism, and thus the T'ang rulers were disposed to treat the Taoist religion with special favor. But because Buddhism enjoyed far greater support among the populace in general than did Taoism, Emperor Wu-tsung was at first obliged to confine his anti-Buddhist sentiments to the area of his own personal life. It was only after he ascended the throne that he was able to employ the power and prestige of the government in carrying out restrictive measures against Buddhism.

As in the case of the earlier persecutions, there was a Taoist adviser to the throne who operated behind the scenes, a man named Chao Kuei-chen who worked in cooperation with the prime minister Li Te-yü to urge the suppression of Buddhism. As a mark of his predilection for Taoism, Emperor Wu-tsung established a Taoist place of worship within the imperial palace, where fasts and other religious observances were carried out. He also ordered that debates be held in the palace between representatives of the

Buddhist and Taoist religions. But since the emperor was already a zealous supporter of the Taoist teachings, there was little likelihood that the Buddhists could gain a fair hearing at debates held in the royal presence.

Another factor complicating the picture was the presence of Uighur military forces in Ch'ang-an and Lo-yang. The Uighurs, a Turkic people of Central Asia, had earlier been invited into China to help put down a rebellion and had remained in the area, conducting themselves in the manner of an occupying army. The country was thus in a state resembling that of wartime.

Against this background of tension and social instability, an edict was issued in 842 calling for the disciplining of Buddhist monks and nuns and decreeing that any monetary wealth or property such as grain stores, fields, or gardens in their possession be turned over to government officials. The following year, all men who had recently entered the Buddhist priesthood were ordered to be taken into custody, and as a result some three hundred or more newly ordained monks were arrested and sent to Ch'ang-an for punishment. Finally, the order went out to melt down all bronze Buddhist images and implements, the metal to be used for new coinage, while iron images were to be made into farm implements, and gold, silver, or pewter images were to be taken over by the government storehouses.

Severe as the persecution was, there was one factor that worked in favor of the Buddhists, namely, the premature death of its perpetrator, Emperor Wu-tsung. In the third month of 846, less than a year after the promulgation of the final edict against Buddhism, Emperor Wu-tsung died at the age of thirty-three. His successor to the throne, Emperor Hsüan-tsung, quickly took measures to halt the anti-Buddhist movement and to assist the religion in efforts to rebuild. It may be noted that Chao Kuei-chen and the other Taoists who had urged Emperor Wu-tsung on in his steps to suppress Buddhism, twelve men in all, were condemned to death.

The fourth of the major Buddhist persecutions, that of the "One Tsung," was carried out in 955 by Emperor Shih-tsung of the Posterior Chou dynasty (951–60), which ruled for a brief time during the period of political chaos following the collapse of the T'ang dynasty in 907. Unlike the earlier persecutions, this was not an attempt to abolish the Buddhist religion outright, but to reform and regulate it and to bring it under strict government control. It forbade the private ordination of monks and nuns, set up a limited number of officially recognized ordination platforms, and decreed that persons wishing to enter the Buddhist clergy must do so under government supervision. In addition, it prohibited the holding of Buddhist services at night and forbade the founding of any new temples. Temples that did not already have official recognition were to be done away with or merged with temples having official recognition.

In other words, the activities of the Buddhist church were to be carried out under careful government surveillance. The move is counted among the major Buddhist persecutions because, from the point of view of Buddhist believers and practitioners, it severely hampered their freedom of activity. Though the Chinese state had on many occasions in the past attempted to intervene in the conduct of religious affairs, these measures of the Posterior Chou made it clear once and for all that the Buddhist Law was to be subservient to the law of the Chinese monarch.

By this time, however, Buddhism in China was showing unmistakable signs of moral and spiritual decline. It had become increasingly worldly in its concerns as the temples and other religious bodies accumulated hidden stores of wealth and became places in which to evade taxation or military conscription rather than associations of persons sincerely seeking religious understanding. Thus in a sense the Buddhist community brought government interference upon itself through its neglect of the true religious spirit.

Though the details are not always clear, in the case of the earlier persecutions it would appear that Buddhism quickly revived after the lifting of the bans on it, and that even while the bans were in effect there were courageous members of the clergy who openly censured the ruler's actions and numerous believers who were willing to die for their convictions. This was particularly true of the persecution carried out under Emperor Wu of the Northern Chou, when members of the Buddhist community fearlessly defied the government authorities. But by the time of the strictures against the religion promulgated in 955 by the Posterior Chou, that fighting spirit seems to have become a thing of the past.

THE CHARACTERISTICS OF CHINESE BUDDHISM

At least in the case of the earlier persecutions, one is struck by the vigor and alacrity with which the religion recovered after the repressive measures were lifted. This suggests that Buddhism had sunk very deep roots within Chinese society. Let us look, for example, at the persecution carried out by Emperor T'ai-wu of the Northern Wei. Emperor T'ai-wu died in 452, and in the tenth month of the same year, Emperor Wen-ch'eng came to the throne and shortly began issuing edicts to prompt the revival of the religion. Thereupon the members of the Buddhist clergy throughout the country who had gone into hiding among the populace during the seven years when Buddhism was outlawed began fervently working to rebuild the religious establishment. As a result of their efforts, by the closing years of the Northern Wei dynasty there were a total of two million monks and nuns in the country and over thirty thousand temples and nunneries.

After the promulgation of the edict encouraging the restoration of Buddhism, the Northern Wei commenced work on the famous stone images in the Yün-kang grottoes near the capital city of Ta-t'ung in northern Shensi, which remain today one of the outstanding works of Chinese Buddhist sculpture. The idea of carving the images was conceived by the eminent monk T'an-yao, who held the post of supervisor of monks and who petitioned Emperor Wen-ch'eng for permission to begin the carving of the giant images. The project was carried out under government sponsorship and was a manifestation of imperial favor toward the Buddhist religion. T'an-yao, having seen how quickly wooden or metal images of the Buddha had been destroyed in the persecution, no doubt wished to produce stone images that would be capable of withstanding any future persecutions, insuring that the populace would never lack representations of the Buddha. The thoroughness with which Emperor T'ai-wu had carried out his persecution of Buddhism may have suggested to T'an-yao and other members of the clergy that Buddhism was in danger of being wiped out entirely in China. It was around this time, we may recall, that the belief that Chinese Buddhism was entering the Latter Day of the Law began to become prevalent in China.

Cave sculptures were being executed in various parts of China at this time, under the influence of Indian and Central Asian Buddhist art. The famous Tun-huang caves in western Kansu, with their countless statues and murals, were already under construction. After the capital of the Northern Wei was moved from T'a-t'ung to Lo-yang in 494, work was begun on a series of cave sculptures at Lung-men just south of Lo-yang. Though the carving of stone images seems to have been a practice of the times, one cannot help feeling that the Buddhist sculptures of Yün-kang were mainly an expression of the awakened religious fervor that followed the persecution of Emperor T'ai-wu.

The second major persecution, that carried out by Emperor Wu of the Northern Chou, was likewise followed by a period of religious resurgence. The Sui dynasty, after terminating Northern Chou rule in 581 and uniting all of China under its control, set about promulgating edicts to encourage the growth of both Buddhism and Taoism. Emperor Wen of the Sui was a man of intense religious fervor, actively promoting the T'ien-t'ai teachings in south China, while taking measures to revive the fortunes of Buddhism in northern China as well. One almost feels that the vigorous flowering of Buddhism that took place during the Sui and T'ang dynasties was traceable to the Buddhist persecutions of the Northern Chou. From that period of oppression, Buddhism rose up with renewed vigor and dedication, its fortunes revived.

No one can possibly condone the type of government oppression that destroys religious art and property and forces believers to abandon their faith or go into hiding. Yet there can be little doubt that such persecution serves to awaken believers to a new consciousness of the value of their beliefs. As we have seen in the case of the Buddhist persecutions in China, many believers are inspired to challenge their oppressors and fight to defend their faith, and when the oppression is ended, to work with renewed zeal to revive the fortunes of their religion. We would do well to keep in mind the lessons that history teaches us in this respect.

The history of the Buddhist persecutions in China demonstrates another important fact about Chinese Buddhism, namely, that it could never rely upon consistent aid or patronage from official circles in spreading its teachings. From very early times, the Chinese emperors exercised virtually absolute authority in their rule. Some among them were ardent Buddhists, but their personal religious convictions constituted no more than one facet of their lives. In almost no cases did they attempt to utilize the full government authority vested in them to promote the spread of Buddhist teachings. In this respect they stand in contrast to the many Christian rulers of Europe who saw themselves as propagators and defenders of the faith. In China, Buddhism spread among the people as the result of the efforts of the local clergy and religious leaders, sometimes with approval from the men in government office, sometimes without it. In fact, it was probably the repeated cycle of government oppression followed by periods of approval that caused the religion to spread from the capital area into the outlying provinces and to take such strong root among the populace as a whole. The two major Buddhist persecutions of the Northern Wei and the Northern Chou, as well as other less striking incidents of harassment and the frequent wars and political disturbances of the time had the effect of disrupting the Buddhist centers in the north and bringing about a spread of Buddhist teachings to the area south of the Yangtze and westward to the remoter regions of Szechwan and the other western provinces.

While northern China was undergoing periods of persecution, causing believers to flee elsewhere for safety, the region south of the Yangtze proved during this period to be generally congenial to the growth of Buddhism. The successive dynasties ruling in the south, perhaps because of their political weakness, did not attempt any official persecution of Buddhism, though the religion was frequently subject to polemical attack. On the contrary, the period saw the appearance of one of the most outstanding imperial patrons of Buddhism in all of Chinese history, Emperor Wu of the Liang dynasty.

Emperor Wu, who reigned from 502 to 549, was an enthusiastic follower of Buddhism and took various measures to encourage the building of temples and the spread of the teachings. Such lavish official patronage, however, did not in all cases prove beneficial to the religion, at times leading to abuses among the religious leaders of the period. Moreover, Emperor Wu's zeal for Buddhism prompted him in 517 to order the abolition of all Taoist temples and the forced return of all Taoist priests to the laity. This measure naturally served to increase the animosity between the two rival religions of Taoism and Buddhism, and obliged many of the Taoist clergy to flee to northern China for safety. Imperial favor could in certain insidious ways be almost as damaging to the health of Buddhism as imperial oppression. In the end, the only healthy growth for the religion was that which came from the fervor of its own leaders and supporters among the populace as a whole.

Whether in spite of persecution or because of it, there is no doubt that Buddhism lasted longer in China and gained a firmer footing within the life and society of the nation than any other foreign creed or system of thought introduced to the country over the three thousand years of its long cultural history. Nestorianism, Zoroastrianism, Islam, and the teachings of Catholic and Protestant Christianity have all been introduced to China at one time or another, but none have had as great or as long-lasting an effect upon Chinese life and thought as has Buddhism. In this respect too, it is unique.

In this volume, we have briefly traced the history of Buddhism during the first thousand years of its propagation in China. A foreign religion introduced from abroad, it probably first attracted attention among the courtiers and members of the aristocracy chiefly because of its exotic flavor. With time it spread to the members of the gentry class and then to the populace as a whole, gradually extending its influence throughout the entire range of Chinese society. Thereafter, influencing and in turn being influenced by Confucianism, Taoism, and the other traditional systems of belief in China, it developed until it had evolved into a distinctively Chinese type of religion with its own institutions and practices. It ceased to be a creed imported from India and Central Asia, and became a body of beliefs expressive of the faith and inner spiritual being of the Chinese people as a whole.

This unique new kind of Buddhism, Chinese Buddhism, then spread to the states of the Korean Peninsula, and from there was transmitted to Japan. And now this religion, which is the faith of so many different peoples across the broad continent of Asia, is in the process of spreading around the entire globe. What the future history of Buddhism will be like it is too soon to tell. But there can be no doubt that, in the process of its past development, the role played by Chinese Buddhism, with its millions of followers down through the centuries, has been one of vast and inestimable importance. If our discussions here have helped to suggest the nature of that role and outlined its principal features, they will have fulfilled their purpose.

Appendices

Maps

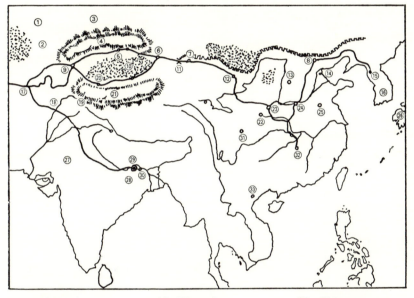

1. K'ang-chü	12. Wu-wei	23. Ch'ang-an
2. Ta-yüan	13. T'ai-yüan	24. Ho-nan (Lo-yang)
3. Wu-sun	14. Po-hai	25. P'eng-ch'eng
4. T'ien-shan Mts.	15. Lo-lang	26. Wo (Japan)
5. Kucha	16. Han	27. Shen-tu (India)
6. Lou-lan	17. Kushan	28. Magadha
7. Tun-huang	18. Yüeh-chih	29. Pataliputra
8. Yü-yang	19. Kashmir	30. Rajagriha
9. Kashgar	20. Khotan	31. Shu
10. Karashahr	21. K'un-lin Mts.	32. Ch'ang-sha
11. Yü-men Kuan	22. Han-chung	33. Chiao-chih

171

II Central Asia during the first and second centuries A.D.

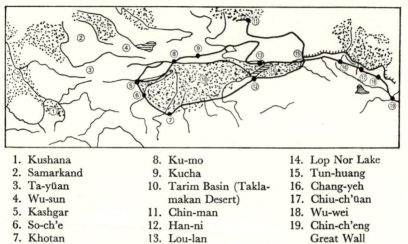

1. Kushana	8. Ku-mo	14. Lop Nor Lake
2. Samarkand	9. Kucha	15. Tun-huang
3. Ta-yüan	10. Tarim Basin (Takla-	16. Chang-yeh
4. Wu-sun	makan Desert)	17. Chiu-ch'üan
5. Kashgar	11. Chin-man	18. Wu-wei
6. So-ch'e	12. Han-ni	19. Chin-ch'eng
7. Khotan	13. Lou-lan	Great Wall

III Central Asia around the fifth century A.D.

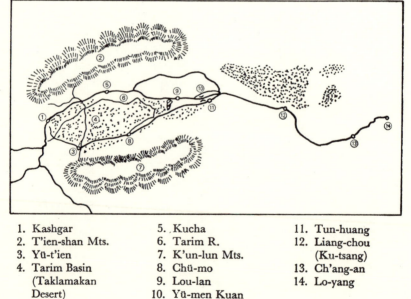

1. Kashgar	5. Kucha	11. Tun-huang
2. T'ien-shan Mts.	6. Tarim R.	12. Liang-chou
3. Yü-t'ien	7. K'un-lun Mts.	(Ku-tsang)
4. Tarim Basin	8. Chü-mo	13. Ch'ang-an
(Taklamakan	9. Lou-lan	14. Lo-yang
Desert)	10. Yü-men Kuan	

IV   Spread of Buddhism in China (Later Han to
end of Six Dynasties Period)

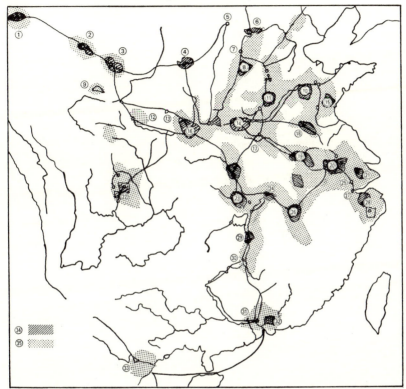

1. Tun-huang	15. Lang-ya	29. Ch'ang-sha
2. Chang-yeh	16. Chung-nan Mts.	30. Mt. Heng
3. Liang-chou	17. Jung-yang	31. Kuang-chou
4. T'ung-wan	18. P'eng-ch'eng	32. Mt. Lo-fou
5. Yün-kang	19. Shou-ch'un	33. Chiao-chih
6. P'ing-ch'eng	20. Chien-k'ang	34. Areas to which
7. Mt. Wu-t'ai	21. Wu	Buddhism had
8. T'ai-yüan	22. Ch'eng-tu	spread by end
9. Hsi-p'ing	23. Chiang-ling	of Chin (419)
10. Mt. T'ai	24. Wu-ch'ang	35. Areas to which
11. Yeh	25. Wu-hsing	Buddhism had
12. Lung-hsi	26. Mt. Lu	spread by end
13. Ch'ang-an	27. Hang-chou	of Six Dynasties
14. Lo-yang	28. Mt. T'ien-t'ai	(588)

V   Route of Fa-hsien's journey to India

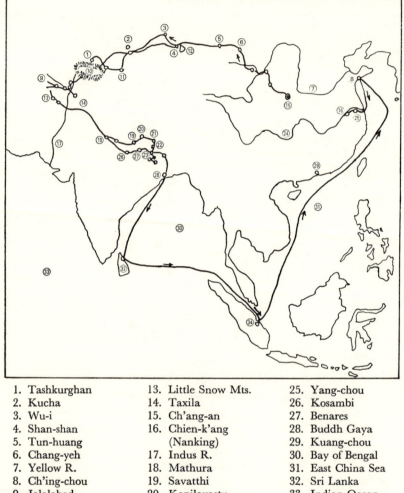

1. Tashkurghan	13. Little Snow Mts.	25. Yang-chou
2. Kucha	14. Taxila	26. Kosambi
3. Wu-i	15. Ch'ang-an	27. Benares
4. Shan-shan	16. Chien-k'ang	28. Buddh Gaya
5. Tun-huang	(Nanking)	29. Kuang-chou
6. Chang-yeh	17. Indus R.	30. Bay of Bengal
7. Yellow R.	18. Mathura	31. East China Sea
8. Ch'ing-chou	19. Savatthi	32. Sri Lanka
9. Jalalabad	20. Kapilavastu	33. Indian Ocean
10. Ts'ung-ling	21. Kushinagara	34. Djambi (Suma-
(Pamir) Mts.	22. Vaishali	tra)
11. Khotan	23. Pataliputra	
12. Lop Nor Lake	24. Yangtze R.	

VI   Places associated with Chih-i's youth

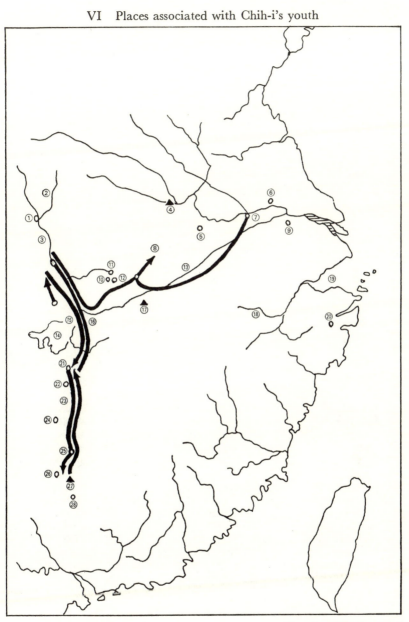

(legend on following page)

(legend for map on preceding page)

1. Hsiang-chou
   (Hsiang-yang)
2. Han R.
3. Chih-i enters
   priesthood at
   Hsiang-chou
4. Mt. Ta-su
5. Lu-chou
6. Chih-i goes to
   Chien-k'ang
7. Chien-k'ang
   (Nanking)

8. Chih-i studies
   under Hui-ssu
9. Ch'ang-chou
10. Han-yang
11. Han-k'ou
12. Wu-ch'ang
13. Yangtze R.
14. Lake Tung-t'ing
15. Hua-jung
16. Chih-i's birth-
    place
17. Mt. Lu

18. Chien-t'ang R.
19. Hangchow Bay
20. Mt. T'ien-t'ai
21. Ch'ang-sha
22. Hsiang-t'an
23. Mt. Heng
24. Heng-chou
    (Heng-yang)
25. Yung-hsing
26. Hsüan-chang
27. Mt. Ta-hsien
28. Mt. Yün-men

1. Samarkand
2. Kashgar
3. Kucha
4. Agni
5. Turfan
6. Hami
7. Lop Nor Lake
8. Yü-men Kuan
   (Jade Gate
   Barrier)
9. Amu-Dar'ya R.
10. Iron Gate
11. Pamir Mts.
12. Calmadana

13. Navapa
14. Bamiyan
15. Ho-p'an-t'o
16. Hindu Kush
    Mts.
17. Kashmir
18. Gandhara
19. Rajapura
20. Kuluta
21. Tibet
22. Indus R.
23. Mathura
24. Ganges R.
25. Kapilavastu

26. Himalaya Mts.
27. Valabhi
28. Benares
29. Pataliputra
30. Kushinagara
31. Vaishali
32. Kamarupa
33. Buddh Gaya
34. Nalanda
35. Rajagaha
36. Kalinga
37. Arabian Sea
38. Kanchipura
39. Sri Lanka

VII   Route of Hsüan-tsang's journey to India

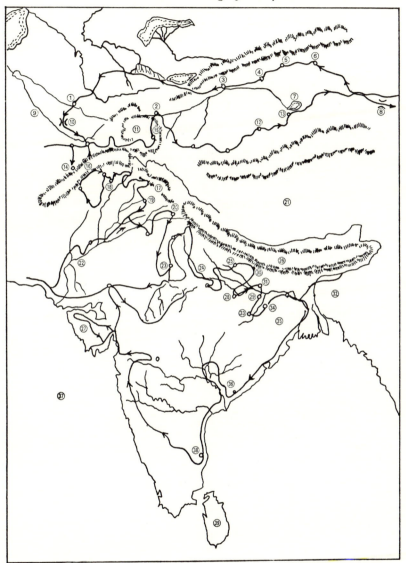

VIII T'ang-dynasty China

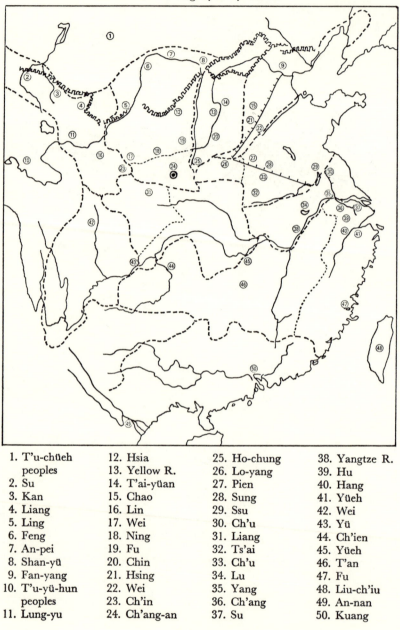

1. T'u-chüeh peoples	12. Hsia	25. Ho-chung	38. Yangtze R.
2. Su	13. Yellow R.	26. Lo-yang	39. Hu
3. Kan	14. T'ai-yüan	27. Pien	40. Hang
4. Liang	15. Chao	28. Sung	41. Yüeh
5. Ling	16. Lin	29. Ssu	42. Wei
6. Feng	17. Wei	30. Ch'u	43. Yü
7. An-pei	18. Ning	31. Liang	44. Ch'ien
8. Shan-yü	19. Fu	32. Ts'ai	45. Yüeh
9. Fan-yang	20. Chin	33. Ch'u	46. T'an
10. T'u-yü-hun peoples	21. Hsing	34. Lu	47. Fu
11. Lung-yu	22. Wei	35. Yang	48. Liu-ch'iu
	23. Ch'in	36. Ch'ang	49. An-nan
	24. Ch'ang-an	37. Su	50. Kuang

Chinese Proper Names

The following is a list of the principal Chinese personal names appearing in the text. A few place names, names of dynasties, and era names have been included as well. The first entry is in Wade-Giles romanization, used in the text. This is followed by the pinyin romanization, the Japanese reading, and English or Sanskrit equivalents where relevant.

Wade-Giles	*Pinyin*	*Japanese*	*Other*
An-hsi	Anxi	Ansoku	Parthia
An-lin	Anlin	Anrin	
An Lu-shan	An Lushan	An Rokuzan	
An Shih-kao	An Shigao	An Seikō	
Chang-an Ta-shih	Zhang'an Dashi	Shōan Daishi	Great Teacher Chang-an
Ch'ang-chieh	Changjie	Chōshō	
Chang Ch'ien	Zhang Qian	Chō Ken	
Chang Pin	Zhang Bin	Chō Hin	
Chan-jan	Zhanran	Tannen	
Chao Kuei-chen	Zhao Guizhen	Chō Kishin	
Chao P'u-ch'u	Zhao Puchu	Chō Bokusho	
Ch'en Chen	Chen Zhen	Chin Shin	
Chia-she Mo-t'eng	Jiashe Moteng	Kashō Matō	
Chien-chen	Jianzhen	Ganjin	
Chien-ch'u-ssu	Jianchusi	Kensho-ji	
Chih Ch'ien	Zhi Qian	Shi Ken	
Chih Fa-tu	Zhi Fadu	Shi Hōdo	

179

Chih-i	Zhiyi	Chigi	
Chih Liang	Zhi Liang	Shi Ryō	
Chih Lou-chia-ch'an	Zhi Loujiachan	Shi Rukasen	Lokaraksha
Chih-meng	Zhimeng	Chimō	
Chih Shih-lun	Zhi Shilun	Shi Seron	
Chih-tsang	Zhizang	Chizō	
Chih-wei	Zhiwei	Chi-i	
Chih-yen	Zhiyan	Chigon	
Chih Yüeh	Zhi Yue	Shi Yō	
Chih-yün	Zhiyun	Chiun	
Ching-hsi Chan-jan	Jingxi Zhanran	Keikei Tannen	
Ching-lu	Jinglu	Keiro	
Chin-kang-chih	Jingangzhi	Kongōchi	Vajrabodhi
Chi-tsang	Jizang	Kichizō	
Chüeh-hsien	Juexian	Kakken	Buddhabhadra
Chu Fa-hu	Zhu Fahu	Jiku Hōgo	
Chu Kao-tso	Zhu Gaozuo	Jiku Kōza	
Chu Shih-hsing	Zhu Shixing	Shu Shikō	
Chu Tao-sheng	Zhu Daosheng	Jiku Dōshō	
Fa-hsien	Faxian	Hokken	
Fa-hsü	Faxu	Hōsho	
Fang-yen	Fangyan	Hōgan	
Fan Yeh	Fan Ye	Han Yō	
Fa-tsang	Fazang	Hōzō	
Fa-yün	Fayun	Hōun	
Fu Chien	Fu Jian	Fu Ken	
Ho Ch'ü-ping	Huo Qubing	Kaku Kyohei	
Hou-chu	Houzhu	Kōshu	
Hsiao-ta	Xiaoda	Kōtatsu	
Hsien-pei	Xianbei	Senbi	
Hsing-man	Xingman	Gyōman	
Hsi Tso-ch'ih	Xi Zuochi	Shū Sakushi	
Hsiung-nu	Xiongnu	Kyōdo	
Hsi-yü	Xiyu	Saiiki or Seiiki	Western Region
Hsüan (emperor)	Xuan	Sen	
Hsüan-lang	Xuanlang	Genrō	

Hsüan-tsang [-chuang]	Xuanzang [-zhuang]	Genjō	
Hsüan-tsung (emperor)	Xuanzong	Gensō	
Hsüan-tsung (emperor, successor to Wu-tsung)	Xuanzong	Sensō	
Huan (emperor)	Huan	Kan	
Hua-ting	Huading	Kachō	
Hui-ch'ang	Huichang	Kaishō	
Hui-chiao	Huijiao	Ekō	
Hui-chien	Huijian	Eken	
Hui-ching	Huijing	Ekei	
Hui-kuan	Huiguan	Ekan	
Hui-kuang	Huiguang	Ekō	
Hui-k'uang	Huikuang	Ekō	
Hui-li	Huili	Eryū	
Hui-ssu	Huisi	Eshi	
Hui-ta	Huida	Etatsu	
Hui-tz'u	Huici	Eji	
Hui-wei (companion of Fa-hsien)	Huiwei	Ekai	
Hui-wei (leader of T'ien-t'ai Sect)	Huiwei	Ei	
Hui-wen	Huiwen	Emon	
Hui-ying	Huiying	Eō	
Hui-yüan	Huiyuan	Eon	
I-ching	Yijing	Gijō	
I-hsing	Yixing	Ichigyō	
I-ts'un	Yicun	Ison	
K'ang-chü	Kangju	Kōkyo	Sogdiana
K'ang Meng-hsiang	Kang Meng-xiang	Kō Mōshō	
K'ang Seng-hui	Kang Senghui	Kō Sōe	
K'ang Seng-k'ai	Kang Sengkai	Kō Sōgai	
Kan Ying	Gan Ying	Kan Ei	

Kao-tsung (emperor)	Gaozong	Kōsō	
K'ou Ch'ien-chih	Kou Qianzhi	Kō Kenshi	
Kuang-che-ssu	Guangzhesi	Kōtaku-ji	
Kuan-ting	Guanding	Kanchō	
K'uei-chi	Kuiji	Kiki	
Lao Tzu	Laozi	Rōshi	
Liang-su	Liangsu	Ryōshuku	
Li Hao	Li Hao	Ri Kō	
Li Po [Pai]	Li Bo [Bai]	Ri Haku	
Li Shih-min	Li Shimin	Ri Seimin	
Li Te-yü	Li Deyu	Ri Tokuyū	
Li Yüan	Li Yuan	Ri En	
Lü Kuang	Lü Guang	Ryo Kō	
Lung-men	Longmen	Ryūmon	
Miao-lo Ta-shih	Miaoluo Dashi	Myōraku Daishi	Great Teacher Miao-lo
Ming (emperor)	Ming	Mei	
Ming-k'uang	Mingkuang	Myōkō	
Nan-shan Tao-hsüan	Nanshan Dao-xuan	Nanzan Dōsen	
Nan-yüeh	Nanyue	Nangaku	
Pan Ku	Ban Gu	Han Ko	
Pao-liang	Baoliang	Hōryō	
Pao-yün	Baoyun	Hōun	
P'ei Sung-chih	Pei Songzhi	Hai Sōshi	
Po Chü-i	Bo [Bai] Juyi	Haku Kyoi [Haku Rakuten]	
Pu-k'ung	Bukung	Fukū	Amoghavajra
Seng-chao	Sengzhao	Sōjō	
Seng-ching	Sengjing	Sōkei	
Seng-jou	Sengrou	Sōjō	
Seng-jui	Sengrui	Sōei	
Seng-shao	Sengshao	Sōshō	
Seng-yu	Sengyou	Sōyū	
Shan-wu-wei	Shanwuwei	Zemmui	Shubhakara-simha

Shih Li-fang	Shi Lifang	Shaku Ribō	
Shih-tsung (emperor)	Shizong	Seisō	
Ssu-ma Ch'ien	Sima Qian	Shiba Sen	
Sun Ch'üan	Sun Quan	Son Ken	
Su-tsung (emperor)	Suzong	Shukusō	
Ta-hsien (mountain)	Daxian	Daiken	
Tai-tsung (emperor)	Daizong	Daisō	
T'ai-tsung (emperor)	Taizong	Taisō	
T'ai-wu (emperor)	Taiwu	Taibu	
T'an-yao	Tanyao	Don'yō	
Tao-an	Daoan	Dōan	
Tao-cheng	Daozheng	Dōshō	
Tao-sui	Daosui	Dōsui	
Ta-su (mountain)	Dasu	Daiso	
T'ien-chu	Tianzhu	Tenjiku	India
T'ien-shih Tao-t'an	Tainshi Daotan	Tenshi Dōdan	
T'ien-t'ai Ta-shih	Tiantai Dashi	Tendai Daishi	Great Teacher T'ien-t'ai
T'o-pa	Tuoba	Takubatsu	
Ts'ui Hao	Cui Hao	Sai Kō	
Tsung Ping	Zong Bing	Sō Hei	
Tu Fu	Du Fu	To Ho	
Tz'u-en Ta-shih	Cien Dashi	Jion Daishi	Great Teacher Tz'u-en
Tzu-kuei	Zigui	Jiki	
Wa-kuan-ssu	Waguansi	Gakan-ji	
Wei Shou	Wei Shou	Gi Shū	
Wei Yüan-sung	Wei Yuansong	Ei Gensū	
Wen (emperor)	Wen	Bun	
Wen-ch'eng (emperor)	Wencheng	Bunsei	
Wu (emperor)	Wu	Bu	

Wu-chung-ssu	Wuzhungsi	Gojū-ji
Wu-tsung (emperor)	Wuzong	Busō
Yang (emperor)	Yang	Yō
Yang Kuei-fei	Yang Guifei	Yō Kihi
Yao Ch'ang	Yao Chang	Yō Chō
Yao Hsing	Yao Xing	Yō Kō
Yen-ts'ung	Yancong	Gensō
Ying (prince)	Ying	Ei
Yü-ch'üan-ssu	Yuquansi	Gyokusen-ji
Yüeh-chih	Yuezhi	Gesshi
Yü Huan	Yu Huan	Gyo Ken
Yün-kang	Yungang	Unkō
Yü-wen	Yuwen	Ubun

Buddhist Texts

The main Buddhist scriptures and other classical works mentioned in the text are given below. The title as it appears in the text, usually in English, serves as the main entry, with Chinese titles (in both the Wade-Giles and pinyin systems of romanization), Japanese titles, and, when appropriate, Sanskrit titles following in that order.

Abhidharmakosha; Chü-she Lun; Jushe Lun; Kusha Ron
Account of Fa-Hsien. See *Record of Buddhist Countries*
Account of the Eminent T'ang Monks Who Journeyed to the Western Regions in Search of the Law; Ta T'ang Hsi-yü Ch'iu-fa Kao Seng Chuan; Da Tang Xiyu Qiufa Gao Seng Zhuan; Dai Tō Saiiki Guhō Kō Sō Den
Agamas; *A-han Ching; Ahan Jing; Agon Kyō*
Annotations on the Mahavairochana Sutra; Ta-jih Ching Shu; Dari Jing Shu; Dainichi Kyō Sho
"Avalokiteshvara" chapter of the *Lotus Sutra; Kuan-shih-yin P'u-sa P'u Men P'in; Guanshiyin Pusa Pu Men Pin; Kanzeon Bosatsu Fumon Bon*
Awakening of Faith in the Mahayana; Ta-ch'eng Ch'i-hsin Lun; Dacheng Qixin Lun; Daijō Kishin Ron

Biographies of Eminent Monks; Kao Seng Chuan; Gao Seng Zhuan; Kō Sō Den
Brief Account of the Wei; Wei Lüeh; Wei Lüe; Giryaku

Chapter on the Grand Meaning of the Mahayana; Ta-ch'eng Ta-i Chang; Dacheng Dayi Zhang; Daijō Daigi Shō
Cheng Fa-hua Ching; Zheng Fahua Jing; Shō Hoke Kyō
Chih-kuan I-li; Zhiguan Yili; Shikan Girei
Chin-kang-p'i Lun; Jin'gangpi Lun; Kongōbei Ron

185

Chin-p'i Lun; Jinpi Lun; Kompei Ron
Collection of Records Concerning the Tripitaka; Ch'u San-tsang Chi-chi; Chu
  Sanzang Jiji; Shutsu Sanzō Kishū

Diamond Sutra; Chin-kang Ching; Jin'gang Jing; Kongō Kyō; Vajrachedika
  Prajnaparamita Sutra
"Duration of Life" chapter of the *Lotus Sutra; Ju-lai Shou Liang P'in;*
  Rulai Shou Liang Pin; Nyorai Juryō Hon

Essentials of the Commentary on Great Concentration and Insight; Chih-kuan
  Fu-hsing Sou-yao Chi; Zhiguan Fuxing Souyao Ji; Shikan Bugyō Sōyō Ki

Fa-hua Hsüan-i Shih-ch'ien; Fahua Xuanyi Shiqian; Hokke Gengi Shakusen
Fa-hua Hsüan-tsan; Fahua Xuanzan; Hokke Gensan
Fa-hua Tsung-yao; Fahua Zongyao; Hokke Shūyō
Fa-hua Wen-chü Chi; Fahua Wenju Ji; Hokke Mongu Ki
Fa-hua Wu-pai-wen Lun; Fahua Wubaiwen Lun; Hokke Gohyakumon Ron
Flower Garland Sutra; Hua-yen Ching; Huayan Jing; Kegon Kyō
Further Biographies of Eminent Monks; Hsü Kao Seng Chuan; Xu Gao Seng
  Zhuan; Zoku Kō Sō Den

General Meaning of Great Concentration and Insight; Chih-kuan Ta-i; Zhiguan
  Dayi; Shikan Tai-i
Great Concentration and Insight; Mo-ho Chih-kuan; Moho Zhiguan; Maka
  Shikan

History of the Former Han; Han Shu; Han Shu; Kanjo
History of the Later Han; Hou Han Shu; Hou Han Shu; Gokanjo
History of the Wei; Wei Shu; Wei Shu; Gisho

Journey to the West; Hsi-yu Chi; Xiyou Ji; Saiyū Ki

Kanzūden; Kan-t'ung Chuan; Gantong Zhuan
Kuang Hung-ming Chi; Guang Hongming Ji; Kō Gumyō Shū
Kuo-ch'ing Pai-lu; Guoqing Bailu; Kokusei Hyakuron

Larger Perfection of Wisdom Sutra; Ta Pan-jo-po-lo-mi-to Ching; Da Banru-
  oboluomiduo Jing; Dai Hannya Haramitta Kyō; Mahaprajnaparamita
  Sutra
Later Introduction to the Lotus Sutra; Fa-hua Ching Hou-hsü; Fahua Jing
  Houxu; Hoke Kyō Gojo

Light-Emitting Perfection of Wisdom Sutra; Fang-kuang Pan-po Ching;
  Fangguang Banruo Jing; Hōkō Hannya Kyō
Li-tai San-pao Chi; Lidai Sanbao Ji; Rekidai Sambō Ki
Liu-tu-chi Ching; Liuduji Jing; Rokudojū Kyō
*Lotus Sutra; Miao-fa Lien-hua Ching; Miaofa Lianhua Jing; Myōhō Renge
  Kyō.* See also *Cheng Fa-hua Ching; T'ien-p'in Miao-fa Lien-hua Ching*

Mahavairochana Sutra; Ta-jih Ching; Dari Jing; Dainichi Kyō
Mahayana Samgraha; She Ta-ch'eng Lun; She Dacheng Lun; Shō Daijō Ron
Ming Fo Lun; Ming Fo Lun; Myō Butsu Ron
*Mo-ho Chih-kuan Fu-hsing-chuan Hung-chüeh; Moho Zhiguan Fuxingzhuan
  Hongjue; Maka Shikan Bugyōden Guketsu*

Nikayas. *See* Agamas
*Nirvana Sutra; Ta-pan Nieh-p'an Ching; Daban Niepan Jing; Daihatsu
  Nehan Gyō; Mahaparinirvana Sutra*

Pan-chou San-mei Ching; Banzhou Sanmei Jing; Hanju Zammai Kyō
"Peaceful Practices" chapter of the *Lotus Sutra; An-lo Hsing P'in; Anluo
  Xing Pin; Anraku Gyō Hon*
*Prajnaparamita Sutra in Eight-Thousand Lines; Tao-hsing Pan-jo Ching;
  Daoxing Banruo Jing; Dōgyō Hannya Kyō*
*Prajnaparamita Sutra of the Benevolent King; Jen Wang Ching; Ren Wang
  Jing; Ninnō Hannya Kyō*
*Profound Meaning of the Lotus Sutra; Fa-hua Hsüan-i; Fahua Xuanyi;
  Hokke Gengi*
P'u-sa Chieh-shu; Pusa Jieshu; Bosatsu Kaisho

Record of Buddhist Countries; Fo-kuo Chi; Fo-guo Ji; Bukkoku Ki
Record of Orally Transmitted Teachings; Ongi Kuden
*Record of the Lineage of the Buddha and the Patriarchs; Fo-tsu T'ung Chi;
  Fozu Tong Ji; Busso Tō Ki*
Record of the Three Kingdoms; San-kuo Chih; Sanguo Zhi; Sangoku Shi
*Record of the Western Region in the Time of the Great T'ang; Ta T'ang
  Hsi-yü Chi; Da Tang Xiyu Ji; Dai Tō Saiiki Ki*
Records of the Historian; Shih Chi; Shi Ji; Shiki
Rules of Discipline in Ten Categories; Shih-sung Lü; Shisong Lü; Jūju Ritsu

Selection of the Time; Senjishō
Separate Biography of the Great Teacher T'ien-t'ai Chih-che of the Sui; Sui

T'ien-t'ai Chih-che Ta-shih Pieh-chuan; Sui Tiantai Zhizhe Dashi Biezhuan; Zui Tendai Chisha Daishi Betsuden

Shuramgama Sutra; Shouleng-yen Ching; Shoulengyan Jing; Shūryōgon Kyō

Significance of the Peaceful Practices Chapter of the Lotus Sutra; Fa-hua Ching An-lo Hsing I; Fahua Jing Anluo Xing Yi; Hoke Kyō Anraku Gyō Gi

"Skillful Means" chapter of the *Lotus Sutra; Fang-pien P'in; Fangbian Pin; Hōben Bon*

Smaller Perfection of Wisdom Sutra; Hsiao-p'in Pan-jo-lo-mi Ching; Xiaopin Banruoluomi Jing; Shōbon Hannya Haramikkyō; Astahashrika Prajnaparamita

Ssu-i Ching; Sii Jing; Shiyaku Kyō

Stages of Yoga Practice; Yü-ch'ieh-shih-ti Lun; Yuqieshidi Lun; Yugashiji Ron; Yogachara-bhumi

Sutra of Infinite Meaning; Wu-liang-i Ching; Wuliangyi Jing; Muryōgi Kyō

Sutra of Meditation on Bodhisattva Samantabhadra; Kuan P'u-hsien P'u-sa Hsing-fa Ching; Guan Puxian Pusa Xingfa Jing; Kan Fugen Bosatsu Gyōhō Kyō

Sutra of the Great Assembly; Ta-chi Ching; Daji Jing; Daishukkyō

Sutra on the Ten Stages; Shih-ti Ching; Shidi Jing; Jūji Kyō; Dashabhumika Sūtra

Ta Tang Ta-tz'u-en-ssu San-tsang Fa-shih Chuan; Da Tang Daciensi Sanzang Fashi Zhuan; Dai Tō Daijionji Sanzō Hōshi Den

T'ien-p'in Miao-fa Lien-hua Ching; Tianpin Miaofa Lianhua Jing; Tembon Myōhō Renge Kyō

Treatise in One Hundred Verses; Pai [Po] Lun; Bai [Bo] Lun; Hyaku Ron

Treatise on the Establishment of the Consciousness-only System; Ch'eng Wei-shih Lun; Cheng Weishi Lun; Jō Yuishiki Ron

Treatise on the Establishment of Truth; Ch'eng-shih Lun; Chengshi Lun; Jōjitsu Ron; Satyasiddhi Shastra

Treatise on the Larger Perfection of Wisdom; Ta-chih-tu Lun; Dazhidu Lun; Daichido Ron

Treatise on the Middle Way; Chung Lun; Zhong Lun; Chū Ron

Treatise on the Ten Stages; Shih-chu P'i-p'o-sha Lun; Shizu Piposha Lun; Jūjū Bibasha Ron

Treatise on the Twelve Gates; Shih-erh Men Lun; Shier Men Lun; Jūni Mon Ron

Tso-ch'an San-mei Ching; Zuochan Sanmei Jing; Zazen Zammai Kyō

Vimalakirti Sutra; Wei-mo Ching; Weimo Jing; Yuima Gyō; Vimalakirti-nirdesha

Wei-mo Ching Lüeh-shu; Weimo Jing Lüeshu; Yuima Gyō Ryakusho

Wen-chü Ssu-chih Chi; Wenju Sizhi Ji; Mongu Shishi Ki

Words and Phrases of the Lotus Sutra; Fa-hua Wen-chü; Fahua Wenju;
Hokke Mongu

Writing Setting Forth My Vow; Li-shih Yüan Wen; Lishi Yuan Wen; Ryūsei
Gan Mon

Buddhist Terms

The main Buddhist terms appearing in the text are listed below. The term as it appears in the text serves as the main entry, usually in English or Chinese (in Wade-Giles romanization), followed by pinyin romanization, Japanese, and, where appropriate, Sanskrit.

Abhidharma teachings; *tsang-chiao; zangjiao; zōkyō*
Ch'an Sect; Chan Sect; Zen Sect
Ch'eng-shih Sect; Chengshi Sect; Jōjitsu Sect
chen-ju sui-yüan; zhenru suiyuan; shinnyo zuien
Chen-yen Sect; Zhenyan Sect; Shingon Sect
connecting teachings; *t'ung-chiao; tongjiao; tsūgyō*
Consciousness-only Sect; Wei-shih Sect; Weishi Sect; Yuishiki Sect;
   Vijnanavada Sect (also, Yogachara Sect)
Correct Law; Cheng-fa; Zhengfa; Shōbō; Former Day of the Law
End of the Law; Mo-fa; Mofa; Mappō; Latter Day of the Law
Fa-hsiang Sect; Faxiang Sect; Hossō Sect
fou-t'u; foutu; futo; Buddha
gradual doctrine; *chien-chiao; jianjiao; zengyō*
hu-seng; huseng; kosō
Imitative Law; Hsiang-fa; Xiangfa; Zōbō; Middle Day of the Law
indeterminate doctrine; *pu-ting-chiao; budingjiao; fujōkyō*
ko-i; geyi; kakugi
Lotus Sutra meditation; *Fa-hua san-mei; Fahua sanmei; Hokke sammai*
nonbeing; *wu; wu; mu*
P'i-t'an Sect; Pitan Sect; Bidon Sect; Abhidharma Sect
round teachings; *yüan-chiao; yuanjiao; engyō*
sang-men; sangmen; sōmon; shramana
San-lun Sect; Sanlun Sect; Sanron Sect

191

secret doctrine; *pi-mi-chiao; bimijiao; himitsukyō*
sha-men; shamen; shamon; shramana
She-lun Sect; Shelun Sect; Shōron Sect
special teachings; *pieh-chiao; biejiao; bekkyō*
sudden doctrine; *tun-chiao; dunjiao; tonkyō*
ten onenesses; *shih-pu-erh-men; shibuermen; jippunimon*
three thousand worlds in one instant of thought; *i-nien san-ch'ien; yinian sanqian; ichinen sanzen*
Ti-lun Sect; Dilun Sect; Jiron Sect
Vinaya; Lü; Lü; Ritsu

Selected Bibliography of Works in English

Ch'en, Kenneth K. S. *Buddhism in China: A Historical Survey*. Princeton: Princeton University Press, 1964.

deBary, Wm. Theodore, Wing-tsit Chan, and Burton Watson, eds. *Sources of Chinese Tradition*. New York: Columbia University Press, 1960.

Hurvitz, Leon, trans. *Wei Shou: Treatise on Buddhism and Taoism*. Kyoto: Kyoto University Press, 1956.

Legge, James, trans. *A Record of Buddhist Kingdoms*. Oxford: Clarendon Press, 1891; New York: Dover Publications, 1962.

Reischauer, Edwin O. *Ennin's Travels in T'ang China*. New York: The Ronald Press Company, 1955.

Reischauer, Edwin O., trans. *Ennin's Diary*. New York: The Ronald Press Company, 1955.

Watters, Thomas, trans. *On Yuan Chwang's Travels in India*. 2 vols. London: Royal Asiatic Society, 1904–5.

Wright, Arthur R. *Buddhism in Chinese History*. Stanford: Stanford University Press, 1959.

Zürcher, E. *The Buddhist Conquest of China*. Leiden: E. J. Brill, 1959.

193

Index

195

The "weathermark" identifies this book as a production of Weatherhill, Inc., publishers of fine books
on Asia and the Pacific. Editorial supervision: Jeffrey Hunter. Cover
design by D.S. Noble. Printed and bound by Royal Book.